This edition published by:-
Oriental Publications
16 Market Street
Adelaide 5000
South Australia

National Library of Australia Cataloguing-in Publication:-
Bibliography.

ISBN 0 9587113 0 5

1. Feng Shui. II. Cheng Hai, Yap. II. Title.

First published July 1993
Second printing February 1994
Third printing June 1994
Fourth printing November 1994
Fifth printing June 1994
Sixth printing August 1995
Seventh printing April 1996
Eighth printing May 1996
Nineth printing February 1997
Tenth printing September 1997

Published by:
NORTH AMERICAN EDITION
Oriental Publications
(Under License from Konsep Lagenda Sdn Bhd)
Copyright: © 1993 Lillian Too

Printed by Ritz Print Sdn. Bhd.

APPLIED

PA-KUA and LO SHU

FENG SHUI

by
Lillian Too

In collaboration with **FENG SHUI MASTER**

YAP CHENG HAI

**ORIENTAL
PUBLICATIONS**

ACKNOWLEDGEMENTS

Writing this SEQUEL to my introductory book on Feng Shui has given me immense pleasure ... and I owe a debt of gratitude to Master Yap Cheng Hai not only for his great generosity in sharing the secret formulas of Pa-Kua Lo-Shu Feng Shui with me and through me, my readers, but also for his patience interpreting and reviewing the formulas with me ...

I also want to express my appreciation to YB Datuk Seri Dr Ling Liong Sik, President of the Malaysian Chinese Association for launching "FENG SHUI" at a Special Conference on the 20th February this year. His support has been invaluable and very encouraging. I also thank him for his generous comments of this Sequel to my first book.

Grateful appreciation is due also to a friend from the old days, well known book reviewer and renowned author, Syed Adam Al-Jafri for writing an excellent Foreword to this sequel, and also to a new friend, Atok Ilhan, the country head of the Phillips Group of Companies, who read my first book ... He has very kindly written a marvellous endorsement of this Sequel for which I am most grateful. To those, whose wonderfully supportive reviews and comments I reproduce within these pages I also extend my thanks ... as well as the hundreds of well wishers and readers of my first FENG SHUI book who wrote to me with splendidly encouraging feedback. I am truly glad Feng Shui has helped them, and I thank them for sharing their experiences with me.

Lillian Too
July 1993

ISBN 0 9587113 0 5
ORIENTAL PUBLICATIONS
Illustrations & Cover Design by Lillian Too
Copyright: ©1993 Lillian Too

WHAT IS
Compass School FENG SHUI ....

Feng Shui is the Art of harnessing Wind and Water. Feng Shui is also about capturing the Dragon's vital cosmic breath or Chi, the force that circulates and moves within the environment, indoors and outdoors, on land, in water, across mountains ....

Chi is everywhere.
Chi is the invisible energy that vibrates through the human body and resonates across the lands of the world, moving, whirling, circulating and ... finally settling. And wherever it settles, or is created, a special kind of energy is released which attracts abundant good fortune, engenders vibrant good health and creates enormous prosperity.

Man's destiny is vastly improved when Chi is captured through the practice of Feng Shui....

In the beginning attention focused on Landscape Feng Shui where emphasis was on the shapes of mountains and the direction of water flows. Over the centuries master practitioners realised Man's destiny could be further enhanced if there was also correct alignment of the environment's Chi to that of the human Chi of the individual.

Thus was Compass School Feng Shui formulated & developed.

This book contains one of the most potent classical formula of the Compass School, one which makes use of the Pa-Kua symbol with its eight trigrams in combination with the Lo-Shu magic square.
This amazing secret formula, extracted from hand-written old texts from the Chien Lung period of the Chin Dynasty has been simplified and thoroughly explained within these pages ...

Use this book to determine YOUR personal directions and to align YOUR individual Chi with that of your environment thereby creating excellent Feng Shui orientations for yourself ......

OTHER BOOKS BY THE AUTHOR

FENG SHUI: THE CHINESE DRAGON
APPLIED PA-KUA and LO SHU FENG SHUI
PRACTICAL APPLICATIONS OF FENG SHUI
CHINESE NUMEROLOGY IN FENG SHUI
WATER FENG SHUI FOR WEALTH
EXPLORE THE FRONTIERS OF YOUR MIND
TAP THE POWER INSIDE YOU
CHINESE ASTROLOGY FOR ROMANCE & RELATIONSHIPS

.... A WELCOME SEQUEL

" Lillian Too's remarkable book on FENG SHUI reveals extraordinary new insights into this ancient Chinese practice and kept me utterly fascinated. Living and working in this part of the world has convinced me Feng Shui is worth investigating; Indeed, I have observed its mysterious forces work in many situations and events and am convinced there IS good and bad Feng Shui. I have also found that much of Feng Shui is straightforward logic which can be beneficially employed by businessmen and career professionals to beget auspicious good luck.

Feng Shui is a complex subject that requires deep knowledge of Chinese metaphysical sciences. Lillian's treatment of the subject in her introductory first book is thorough and comprehensive. Her second book is thus a welcome SEQUEL.

In this SEQUEL, she delves deeper into the subject, and focuses on Compass School formulations and methods that have been extracted from ancient texts. These techniques use individual birth dates to determine auspicious & unfavourable directions. This Sequel is titled "APPLIED PA-KUA LO-SHU FENG SHUI" as these two powerful Chinese symbols feature prominently in the formulas.

Lillian Too writes in an appealing and readable style. Both books are cleverly arranged and fully illustrated to make comprehension easy and fun. The books also entertain the reader with charming real life and business anecdotes.

I strongly recommend "FENG SHUI" and "APPLIED Pa-Kua Lo-Shu FENG SHUI" to Western cultured residents and would-be residents of Malaysia and the Far East ! Knowing Lillian and judging by the excellent quality of her first book, I am convinced the SEQUEL offers exciting new knowledge into Feng Shui's practical applications. "

Mr. Atok Ilhan,
Chief Executive, PHILLIPS GROUP OF COMPANIES in MALAYSIA,
President, Malaysian International Chamber of Commerce & Industry.

☆ ☆ ☆ ☆   COMMENTS on "FENG SHUI"   ☆ ☆ ☆ ☆ ☆

"Lillian Too's FENG SHUI is outstanding and spellbinding in more ways than one. Here is a piece of work that has been well researched and represents what the writer has "soaked up" from books and practitioners. The well matched "marriage" between theory and practice contributes to the comprehensiveness of the book. Yet, there is no false pretensions on the part of the writer who warns that studying Feng Shui for personal use is one thing but "checking out' the Feng Shui of someone else's house or office is another matter. A reader's interest is sustained throughout the book, given the simple but clear and precise style of writing, the conversational tone of the discourse and the effective illustrations, not forgetting the interesting Feng Shui anecdotes. FENG SHUI by Lillian Too is a book highly recommended for the practitioner who wish to gain further insights, as well as the non practitioner who wants a good introduction to Feng Shui."
Dr Leong Yin Ching. B.Econs Hons; M.Ed.(Mal); PhD(Lon); A.L.A (Lon)
Professor of Education, University of Malaya.

" HIGHLY READABLE ... and with interesting anecdotes, FENG SHUI should interest everyone who seeks to understand the forces of Nature ... it is an invaluable addition to the growing literature dealing with Eastern thinking, perceptions and Lillian Too should be congratulated for her timely contribution"
Dr Tarcisius Chin,
Chief Executive, Malaysian Institute of Management.

"Lillian Too's books are masterful compilations of the philosophy as well as the practice of this ancient Chinese convention, cleverly updated and beautifully illustrated for the modern day reader ...."
Puan Shahreen Kamaluddin, Managing Director, Shahreen Corporate Communications.

" Lillian Too's books on FENG SHUI are without a doubt exceptionally useful additions to any businessman's library ..."
G. Gnanalingam, Managing Director, G-Team Consultants.
President, Harvard Business School Club of Malaysia.

" ...Lillian's research is a most welcome addition to the fast growing body of literature on FENG SHUI written in English ..."
Dr Ken Yeang. PhD (Cantab). President, Malaysian Institute of Architects 1983 - 1985

"...Be prepared for wonderful new insights into the Chinese mind ... and a totally new perspective to doing business in Asia ..."
Stuart Gordon, MBA (Harvard) President, Kaiser Rollmet, Irvine, California.

✶ COMMENTS ON "APPLIED PA-KUA LO-SHU FENG SHUI" ✶

" This Sequel to Lillian Too's successful "FENG SHUI" is the result of intensive collaboration between the author and Yap Cheng Hai, well known Feng Shui Master. Exciting new Feng Shui insights and "secrets" have emerged.

APPLIED FENG SHUI offers practical and detailed information which promises easy application methods for those who want to seriously improve the Feng Shui of their dwellings and work places. At the same time the author has gone deeper into the philosophical fundamentals of Chinese cultural conventions, at least in so far as they impact on the perceptions and comprehension of Feng Shui. This aspect of her book provides valuable background information to the understanding of the Chinese mind. As such I wish to commend Lillian Too for this insightful guide which will prove useful to those who wish to further advance their understanding of Feng Shui. "

YB. Datuk Seri Dr. Ling Liong Sik,
Minister of Transport, Malaysia,
President, Malaysian Chinese Association.

" A masterful second book on Feng Shui ! This Sequel contains amazing Compass School secret formulas extracted from handwritten old texts that were written down during the Chin Dynasty's Chien Lung period. Once again Lillian Too offers a book filled to overflowing with significant fresh information on the practice of FENG SHUI. The formulations contained in this book are based on the eight sided Pa Kua and the legendary nine chamber Lo Shu magic square. For those who enjoyed her first book FENG SHUI, and found it useful, this SEQUEL is a definate must ... ! "

Yet Ling, Editor-in Chief,
Chinese "WOMEN" magazine.

" From a "kwei-lo's" perspective, Lillian Too's APPLIED FENG SHUI is a magnificent follow up to her exciting first book on Feng Shui. Her insightful accounts of Chinese practice and belief deserve extravagant praise and I soundly applaud her obviously well researched work ! "

David Lee Sherman,
International Legal Counsel, DIBB, LUPTON & BROOMHEAD, London.

CONTENTS

CHAPTER THREE: PA-KUA LO-SHU FENG SHUI

CHAPTER FOUR: FORMULA APPLICATIONS

USING THE PA-KUA DIRECTIONS

USING THE LO-SHU LOCATIONS

CHAPTER FIVE: CASE STUDIES on FORMULA USE

CHAPTER SIX: FENG SHUI DIMENSIONS

CHAPTER SEVEN: IMPROVING YOUR LIFE

CHAPTER EIGHT: THE CHINESE HOROSCOPE

MAN
and his ENVIRONMENT
must HARMONISE

This is an age old wisdom that advocates equilibrium and symmetry with the world's landscapes, its mountains and rivers, its winds and its waters.

The Chinese practice of FENG SHUI encapsulates this in a broadbased body of principles that promises prosperity and abundance, peace and serenity, health and longevity to those who live according to its guidelines of harmony & balance. It is a beneficial component of Chinese culture.

FENG SHUI is Chinese Geomancy, and Lillian Too's books on this centuries old Chinese practice is timely and topical. Certainly the Chinese throughout South East Asia, Hong Kong & Taiwan are fervent practioners of FENG SHUI, especially those in business who want an "extra edge" in the form of Feng Shui "luck".... Like many of my fellow Malaysians of Chinese origin, I am only too familiar with the importance of orienting one's home according to good Feng Shui precepts.

Lillian's books are convincing, thoroughly researched and extremely comprehensive. Classical explanations extracted from ancient manuals, are freely interspersed with hundreds of useful tips and plenty of business anecdotes picked up from her many years of business experience.

I am very pleased to recommend "FENG SHUI" and "APPLIED FENG SHUI" to Malaysians and visitors alike; for those who want an introduction to the subject, and for those who want authentic comprehensive reference books on the subject.

YB.Datuk Seri Dr. Ling Liong Sik,
President, Malaysian Chinese Association
Minister of Transport, Malaysia.

FOREWORD

With characteristic intellectual generosity, the Author invited me to contribute a Foreword to her masterful second book on FENG SHUI. I accepted because fear of any shortcomings on my part was overcome by the prospect that I should learn something beneficial in the process.

And in my limited view, this is the attraction of her two books which bridge linguistic, cultural, and philosophical gaps in a world pushed into electronic and spacial closeness; where human understanding seems to have fallen behind dangerously and sadly.

FENG SHUI offers an integrated set of guideposts that transcend the limitations of culture and civilisation along the road to spiritual maturity. For too long, the wisdom of the ancient Chinese sages have been circumscribed by being accessible almost exclusively, only to the Chinese people (barring a few foreign scholars) and to societies heavily influenced by Chinese cultural practices - Korea, Japan, Taiwan, Hong Kong, Singapore ...

Now in an age of incredible growth in universal and worldwide linkages, it is Lillian Too's considerable achievement to have transposed and elucidated the linguistically-locked knowledge, philosophy and practices of FENG SHUI with such clarity, yet not losing the essence, into the most widely used language of today's (and probably tomorrow's) world.

This is a continuation of the fundamental consistencies of society and world civilisation, from times lost in the misty past to the the present day. I am reminded by her effort of people such as Averroes, (the twelfth century Arabic writer Abu-al-Walid Muhd) and Carl Gustav Jung, the Swiss psycho-analyst. Averroes it was who inquired into the possibility of a "world soul" and sought to bring together Greek and Islamic philosophical thought. Carl Jung and his concept of the "collective unconscious" in various societies, cultures and civilisations, pioneering analytical psychology before studying anthropology and the occult, to produce his theory of archetypes - universal symbols existing within the collective unconscious of all societies.

And here we are nearly touching the cosmogenic theories of Albert Einstein, probing the deep forces of the Universe which affect our world even without most of us realising it.

FENG SHUI is not a subject easily lent to "logical analysis". It demands, at least initially, a certain degree of belief and acceptance of its fundamentals. Viewed from this perspective, the world's people may be categorised into three groups in relation to this Chinese pseudo scientific wisdom.

The first group are those who believe in FENG SHUI with a committment derived from acceptance with (or even without) an understanding of it. Their advantage is the integration of such belief in their observation and decision patterns.

The second group are unbelievers mainly driven by some variety of (western) scientific logic. Professionally, some amongst this group find FENG SHUI unacceptable either as a schematised idea or as a set of principles. They thus categorically reject FENG SHUI as spiritually alien and scientifically absurd !

It is the third group who stand most to gain from this book; people who are (some would say, happily) as yet completely unaware of FENG SHUI due in part to their agnosticism, believing that Man cannot know about things beyond the realm of un-systematised experience. They, for the most part remain closed off, rather than rejectionist and are generally open to being motivated and to learn. This group may be persuaded, once the barriers of language and culture have been surmounted by books such as this, particularly when transcribed by an author whose credibility is solid, and whose study and research into the subject impressively unites profound comprehensive thought with practical analyses.

FENG SHUI seems to be representative of Chinese "Science" in the same manner that the electro-magnetic spectrum is representative of Western Science. In the latter phenomena, visible light emissions constitute only a tiny part of the entire known electro-magnetic spectrum. The rest of the spectrum, from the very shortest to the very logest "waves" is generally invisible to the human eye; yet has been widely accepted as existing.

Invisibility in this case has not been a cause for denial or rejection.

Taking Chi (lines of force; energy, earth currents or more picturesquely, "cosmic dragon's breath"); and FENG SHUI, these provide yet to be discovered dynamic energies and forces on a scale between Earth and Universal manifestation, much like the phenomena manifested through appliances and instruments in the electro-magnetic spectrum.

FENG SHUI's potency and visible effects is thus akin to the technological harnessing of electro-magnetic energies seen in modern gadgets like microwave ovens and CD players and in radios and television sets ... And just as these E-M emissions can be productive and destructive, so too can Chi and FENG SHUI produce beneficial and disastrous results.

What the Chinese colourfully construe as good and bad luck !

To the non-Chinese reader, the prevalence of Chinese popular folklore, myths and beliefs, anecdotes and grassroot interpretation may be a source of added interest; and the creative non Chinese reader of Lillian Too's works will no doubt find parallels in his/her own cultural milieu and folk wisdom.

This book is thus a wonderful starting point on a journey into the boundless, assisting the reader to comprehend Mankind and even perhaps influence, through the practice of Feng Shui, whatever it brings; to understand the highs and lows of Life, and conceivably to come to terms with each vital moment.

Tuan Syed Adam Aljafri.
BA Hons & MA (Yale). Msc(Economics) (London)
Petaling Jaya 1993

Syed Adam was a diplomat at the United Nations; and was formerly Secretary in, & Adviser to Bank Negara Malaysia (the Central Bank) and Professor of Economics & Management in the University of Samoa. He is presently a Management Consultant in his own firm and is a Director of Paramount Berhad and Kolej Damansara Utama, a leading private educational institution. Syed Adam is also a prolific and successful writer of short stories; and occasionally contributes book reviews & articles to the New Straits Times.

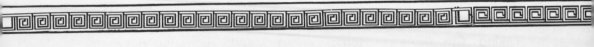

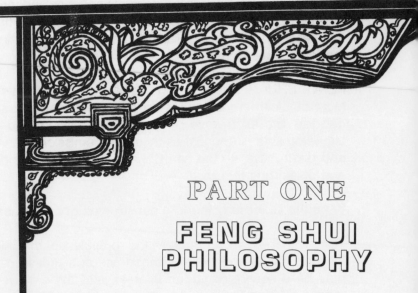

PART ONE

FENG SHUI PHILOSOPHY

CHAPTER ONE

FENG SHUI'S BASIC CONCEPTS

Feng Shui finds beautiful expression in the flows of invisible energy that gently waft through the earth and the sky, floating on its waters, carried along by gentle breezes, bringing abundant happiness and prosperity wherever it circulates and settles ...

The Chinese refer to this energy as *Chi.*

Think of unseen delicate forces moving through the human body and the environment, invisible and unnoticed, yet ever potent. Very similiar to radio waves, telephone signals, radar, magnetic vibrations ... Yoga practitioners allude to "Prana", the inner breath that mysteriously energises the human body, giving a strange sort of strength, an extraordinary kind of vigour.

To the Chinese, Chi is the mysterious inner energy which gives strength and soul to mankind. Chi is created when a monk sits in deep meditation and expertly controls his breathing; each time a kung fu master delivers a well-aimed blow; when the artist calligrapher makes an exquisite brushstroke. In each of these activities a special kind of inner vitality accompanies the movement to create a unique power, a life force that chaperons the breathing, the blow, and the brushstroke, making each of these actions distinctive and superior. These are manifestations of human Chi.

In Feng Shui, Chi is the ever-present force that circulates and moves in the environment. Indoor and outdoor. On land, in water, across mountains ... Chi is everywhere. Chi is the invisible energy that vibrates across the lands of the world, moving, whirling, and dispersing, or circulating and settling ... and wherever Chi settles it brings with it a special kind of energy that attracts extreme good luck.

Feng Shui, or the Art of harnessing "wind and water" is all about capturing or creating Chi. The ancients refer to Chi as the Dragon's cosmic breath, assigning to it magical connotations expressed in lyrical terms. Chinese literature is rich with extraordinary explanations of how balance and harmony in the environment creates a wealth of Chi flows. They attributed the caprices of Heaven and Earth together with their effects on the destinies of mankind to these invisible currents. Thus did the Chinese view their fates as being inextricably entwined with the creative and destructive powers of Nature.

In the process they inevitably sought explanations in the lay of the land, the way rivers flowed and mountain ranges stood. And they compared much of Nature's landscapes to animistic powers - dragons, tigers, phoenixes and tortoises - and how these, in particular the celestial dragon - inhaled and exhaled Chi, the vital life enhancing energy.

It was believed that Chi was the power that created the landscapes of the world, its mountains and rivers, its hills and valleys. Chi determines the shapes and forms and colours of the environment, as well as the health of plants and trees, and all the living creatures within, including Man.

In Man, Chi is the spirit that governs human behaviour and activity. The excellence of its glow (or lack of it) within the mortal body is what determines the health and vitality of the person. The ancients sought to attain perfection by balancing internal Chi so that its flow through the body is smooth and unimpeded, creating in the process an aura of vibrance and energy.

Human Chi differs in quantity and quality from person to person. Often Chi currents get blocked, causing ailments that cause negative outcomes. Thus techniques were developed to enhance human Chi, through meditation, kung fu martial arts exercises or special controlled breathing.

Enhancing human Chi alone was deemed insufficent. One also had to live in harmony with the environment. Thus the Chi of the human body had to be in harmony with the Chi of one's surroundings. Household Chi and Human Chi had to flow smoothly, one in rhythm with the other. Today we know that this harmonious interaction of the two kinds of Chi defines what good Feng Shui is all about.

Feng Shui means living in compatibility with one's environment, fitting comfortably into the place we call home, feeling relaxed and full of the vital life force. Thus can Feng Shui bring abundance and good fortune.

Initially, Feng Shui prescribed basic guidelines to identify locations where maximum landscape Chi exists.

The oldest references to this originated from the Tang Dynasty, around the time of the 9th century when the brilliant Imperial Court adviser, Master Yang Yun Sang authored a series of books which laid down specific guidelines on Landscape Feng Shui. His emphasis was on the shape of mountains and the direction of water courses.

Over the centuries however, practitioners must have realised that equally important to Man's destiny was surely the alignment of the environment's Chi to the human Chi of the individual. The alignment of one's body had surely to complement the alignment of one's home, such that there would be compatibility between Landscape (or Household) Chi with Human Chi. Only thus surely, could the full benefits of Feng Shui be captured.

Thus did Compass School Feng School follow from the discoveries of Form School Feng Shui. The latter, with its colourful animal symbolisms and its stress on the Green Dragon White Tiger formations explained landscape formations in terms of Chi currents, deeming a place as having "good" or "bad" Feng Shui depending on the way hills were placed relative to each other and how rivers flowed.

It was many generations later before Compass School Feng Shui attempted to relate Landscape Chi flows with the Chi flows of the human body. This later method laid stress on correlating the individual's Horoscope and its attendant characteristics and Elements, with the curents of Chi in the Earth's environment.

This second School made use of the eight sided Pa-Kua symbol with its eight Trigrams, and, combining it with the Lo-Shu magic square, devised a method of formulating directions which best matched the individual to his environment.

These formulations became the basis for designing Yang dwellings (ie homes and rooms and work places in the modern context), the placement of rooms for different members of the family, the compass orientations of doors and bedrooms, kitchens and entrances; and even the directions of travels and relocations. Much of the reasoning behind these formulations were based on the way the Lo-Shu magic square was superimposed onto the Later Heaven Pa-Kua thereby matching numbers with compass directions.

From the master practitioners of the Compass School came the invention of the Luo-Pan, generally referred to as the Chinese Geomancer's Compass. To the layman however, the use of the Compass (and there are several different versions of this Compass) requires detailed knowledge of too many intricate and complex inter-relationships. Interpreting the symbolisms of the Elements, the "stars", and the directions, the "Heavenly Stems" and the "Earthly Branches", which make up the content of the many rings of the Geomancer's Compass usually becomes too formidable a task for the layman practitioner.

A more practical approach towards interpreting Compass School formulations is thus recommended. This has led to a step by step simplification of the formulations which have been transformed into easy reference Tables. From these Tables the interested practitioner may then:

1. Determine the relevant auspicious and inauspicious directions and locations from the various Tables given.
2. Make a brief study of the basic concepts and fundamental philosophies of Feng Shui, thereby ensuring at least an understanding of the basic principles that led to the formulation of these Tables in the first place.
3. Familiarise oneself with the authentic Luo-pan before using a modern day Westerner's magnetic compass to determine directions.
4. Study the various permutations and combinations in the application process. Much of Feng Shui practice lies in the interpretation of techniques and guidelines given. Correct interpretation is aided by a sound knowledge of the related influences of the various symbols.

Before proceeding to the actual method and Tables therefore, it is useful and necessary to spend some time understanding the major background influences and origins of Feng Shui practice ie the Chinese Ganzhi System, the Five Elements, the I Ching philosophies, the Pa Kua Trigrams and the Lo-Shu magic square ...

THE LUO-PAN and the GANZHI SYSTEM

The Luo-Pan is an elaborately detailed instrument comprising 24 concentric rings drawn round a small magnetic compass. The inner rings of the Luo-Pan shows the eight trigrams & orientations. The rings that follow display the Heavenly (or Celestial) Stems and the Earthly (or Terrestrial) Branches. These are terms used in the Ganzhi system. For the general practice of Feng Shui it is necessary to acknowledge that the secrets of the Chinese Pa-Kua's significance to Feng Shui as well as the markings of the Luo-Pan cannot be fully understood without at least some knowledge of the Ganzhi system.

This system is packed with cyclic symbols mainly associated with animals, and with the Elements. Basically, Ganzhi comprises 22 symbols which are broadly grouped into two sets, 10 belonging to the Celestial Stems, and 12 belonging to the Terrestrial Branches.

The Stems refer to the Elements, with a "hard" and a "soft" aspect for each, also referred to as Yin and Yang aspects. The Elements are also represented by the Pa-Kua's four Celestial animals, ie the Black Tortoise (North); the Crimson Phoenix (South); the Green Dragon (East) and the White Tiger (West). The centre fifth point is occupied by the Yellow Dragon. The Five Elements and their associated Four Celestial Animals represent an ancient knowledge of how Heavenly forces can be manipulated to affect Earthly destinies, hence Form School Feng Shui.

The Branches, on the other hand refer to Earthly forces, and this is represented by the twelve animals of the Zodiac, the rat, the ox, the tiger, the rabbit, the dragon, the snake, the horse, the goat(or sheep), the monkey, the rooster, the dog and the boar (or pig).

It is believed that the interactions of the these 22 symbols control everything in the Universe. Hence their significance in understanding Feng Shui and the Chinese explanantions of how Compass Feng Shui works. The ten Celestial Stems are said to reflect the influence of Heavenly forces, and these relate to the Five Elements as disposed according to the Four primary directions of the Compass. The twelve terrestrial Branches apply to the factors on the Earth (the animal symbols) and these are applied to the twelve two hour units of

THE EARLIER LUO-PAN

THE LUO-PAN reproduced here has sixteen "rings". The markings apply to several divination systems. In the centre is the magnetic compass located in the "heaven pool". Around it are the eight Trigrams arranged in the Former Heaven Sequence. From thence on the Luo-Pan proceeds to depict the 24 "compass points" corresponding to Stems and Branches, with reference in later rings to the Elements, and specifically defined lucky and unlucky degrees (or directions). This illustration is for readers' information only; Feng Shui Masters who practise the Compass Method (of ascertaining "lucky" and "unlucky" compass points) usually base their formulations on the Later Heaven Sequence Arrangement of the eight Trigrams.

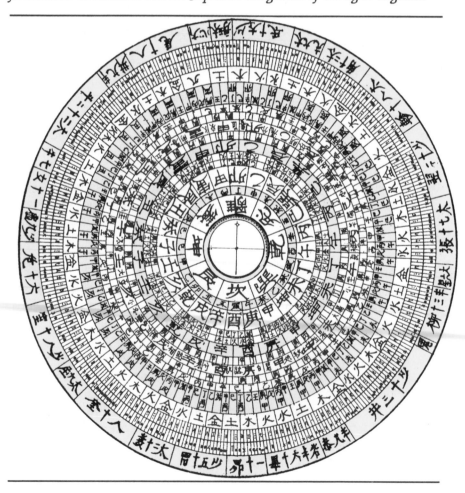

a 24 hour day, the twelve months of the year, and the twelve years corresponding to the twelve zodiac animals. These twelve years, when permutated with the five elements (12 x 5) produce the sixty year cycle. The cycle is repeated every 60 years. The Chinese believe that the Terrestrial Branches interfacing with the Celestial Stems marks the location of the Earth Dragon's "Chi" forces, hence the potency of Compass School Feng Shui which uses the Pa-Kua and the Lo-Shu (corresponding to the Later Heaven Arrangement of the Trigrams). More, the combination of the Branches and the Stems comprehensively signifies the interactions of Heavenly and Earthly forces in the regulation of everything in the life of mankind. Indeed, the ancients know that the Ten Celestial Stems and the Twelve Earthly Branches rule the entire destiny of Man.

The Ganzhi system's two parallel structure of Stems and Branches form the basis of Chinese Astrology. In addition, based on centuries of observation, the Chinese have worked out associations between environmental changes and the lunar, seasonal and solar periods in the sixty year cycles of the Ganzhi system. This is the basis of the Chinese Almanac or Tong Shu, under which, predictions can be made 60 years ahead of time, about the general characteristics of a period through its position in the Ganzhi system.

In Feng Shui, the Ganzhi System's influence is observed through the placement and use of its symbols within the Geomancer's Luo-Pan. At the same time the central importance of the Pa-Kua with its associated symbols, and the special placings of numerals according to the Lo Shu square, are indicative of the mutual dependence of Heaven and Earth forces in matters relating to destiny. One does not exert a greater influence than the other.

In this context it is relevant to remind readers that Man's Destiny is a function of three types of forces or "luck". There is the Heavenly Luck (Tien Chai) which governs whether one is born rich or poor, clever or ignorant and destined for honour or shame; There is also the Earth Luck (Ti Chai) which regulates these same outcomes except that they are determined by the forces of the Earth; and finally there is Man's Luck (Ren Chai) which refers to one's own actions and character determining one's destiny. Feng Shui, seen in this context takes on its true perspective. Feng Shui (representing Ti Chai) represents one of the forces that determine destiny. Good Feng Shui alone does not guarantee abundance or success, but it can help improve destiny.

THE MODERN LUO-PAN

The modern Luo-Pan demonstrates the evolution of the basic rings of the Compass. In the centre is the magnetic needle which indicates South. Immediately circling the centre are eight directions of the Compass with the corresponding Trigrams, this time arranged in the Later Heaven Sequence. The Elements are marked in the next ring. Thus East (numbers 1 and 2) is Wood; South, (numbers 3 and 4) is Fire; West (7 and 8) is Metal while North (9 and 10) is Water. These numbers are the Heavenly Stems. Stems 5 and 6 representing Earth symbolises the centre and is not shown on the rings, indicating a different interpretation of the Trigram/Element connection. Following the Stems come the twelve Earthly Branches. This Luo-Pan closely reflects the influence of the Ganzhi System on Compass Feng Shui. For the layman, using the Luo-Pan can be very confusing unless accompanied by deep knowledge of the many permutations between Trigrams, Stems and Branches, and their corollary, the interactions of Element and the Horoscope influences. It is easier to work from pre-formulated Tables already simplified by the Masters.

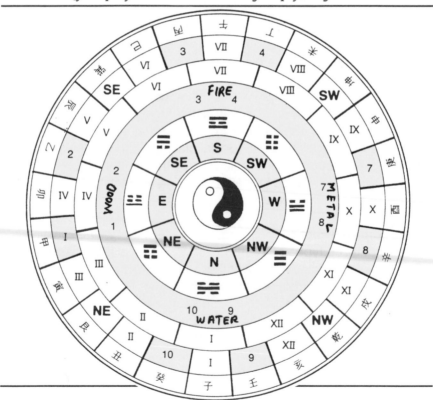

26

SYMBOLISM OF THE FIVE ELEMENTS

The significance of interactions between Heavenly Stems and Earthly Branches on individual destinies is the core of most patterns of Chinese Fortune Telling.

In Compass School Feng Shui, a person's year of birth is also used to determine the governing Pa-Kua number (referred in the book as the KUA number) and from this number, it is then possible to determine the matching Trigrams or Lo-Shu numbers which exemplify best and worst orientations for the person.

Along with these guidelines, it is also possible to determine corresponding Elements, ie Water, Wood, Fire, Metal or Earth from one's horoscope. These Five Elements represent an additional dimension to the practice of Feng Shui simply because it is believed that these Elements, in their inter-actions, indicate an extra way of analysing and harmonising the Chi of a person vis-a-vis his/her house.

Each of the Elements portray some aspect of Chi, in the same way as they also epitomise colours, times, seasons, directions, planets, parts of the body and so forth. Undertaking an in-depth study and analyses of how these Elements interact with each other considerably enhances the practice of Feng Shui.

Application of Element analyses can be approached from several perspectives, each one highlighting one of its symbolisms, ie the colour it represents or the season indicated, or the direction represented and so forth.

Superimposed upon this body of symbolisms are the two primary cycles of the Elements, one the Productive (Positive, Creative) Cycle, and the other, the Destructive (Negative) Cycle.
In a fixed order, and working within a circular flow, each of the Elements "creates or produces" another Element, while at the same time "destroying" another.

Understanding these cycles and then employing them (symbolically) in one's daily life; like in the siting of rooms or the selection of colour combinations, or the extension of homes strongly reinforces other Feng Shui endeavours.

THE PRODUCTIVE CYCLE

In the productive or creative cycle:

FIRE produces EARTH (ash)
EARTH produces METAL (minerals)
METAL produces WATER
WATER produces WOOD (plants)
WOOD produces FIRE

This Productive Cycle is usually depicted in a circular flow as shown in the sketch above. To determine the

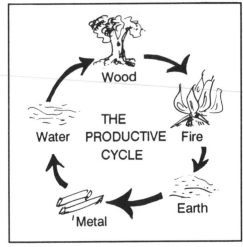

The Productive Cycle.

quality of Feng Shui compatabilities within the house, a person should first have full knowledge of the various Elements that characterise his Horoscope, the most important of which is the Element that governs his/her Year of Birth. This is included in the tabulation of KUA numbers shown in Table 1 of Chapter Three.

There are also Elements associated with one's hour of birth, and an extract of this information taken from the Almanac is reproduced in the Table on the left.

You are now in possession of two of the important Elements you were "born with". Armed with this information your first and most simple analyses is to see whether one of these Elements produce the other; or are nuetral; or are destructive of the other.

Some-times both the hour and year of birth indicate the same Element, and this can be interpreted as there being an excess of that Element in the birth-chart. Traditional Chinese usually investigate further to determine their Elements for month and day of birth as

THE ELEMENT OF BIRTH TIMES

11pm to 1am = WOOD
1am to 3am = WOOD
3am to 5am = FIRE
5am to 7am = FIRE
7am to 9am = EARTH
9am to 11am = EARTH
11am to 1pm = METAL
1pm to 3pm = METAL
3pm to 5pm = WATER
5pm to 7pm = WATER
7pm to 9pm = WATER
9pm to 11pm = WATER

well. If the reader is interested, the author recommends that reference be made to a basic Chinese Astrology Book which offers Tables that reveal the corresponding Elements based on details of one's birth dates and times. This is generally referred to as one's "Paht Chee" or "Eight characters".

Tradition bound families often select names on the basis of "Element" evaluation. Thus, if one is born in a WOOD year, then some WATER featured in the name is supposed to be auspicious for the child since WATER produces WOOD. While this is all well and good, it has also been pointed out to the author that it is sometimes necessary to temper this practice with a certain amount of common-sense.

Thus, while WATER may be good for WOOD, too much WATER will overwhelm WOOD. Take for instance the case of the businessman, born in a WOOD year. Quite rightly, his father put WATER in his name. But the name given was "Tua Hai" (Hokkien for "Big Sea") - definately a case of too much WATER. The sea (Water) will surely engulf the little plant (Wood) !!

When however the hour and year of birth are also WOOD, then it can be interpreted that there is too much WOOD; there is therefore no necessity to produce any more, and hence no necessity to include WATER in the name. A more extreme case is where a child is born with all his "Eight characters" symbolising a single Element. There is then definately too much, in which case it may be required to destroy some of it by including in the child's name, the Element which controls it. In our example of the WOOD child, the reader will note later on that METAL chops (or destroys) WOOD, thus the inclusion of say, gold ("Kim") representing METAL in the name will temper the effects of too much WOOD. Do remember however that too much METAL could also be detrimental.

The interpretations of the Productive Cycle must therefore take cognisance of the need for harmony and balance. According to ancient Chinese belief, everything boils down to balance.

This is overwhelmingly stressed in the Book of Changes or I-Ching, the ancient Chinese Classic from which much of Chinese divination sciences (including Feng Shui) is taken.

Balance, as it relates to the Elements seem to suggest that ideally, the presence of all five Elements is conducive to auspicious Feng Shui, with perhaps some emphasis on the Element that best serves one's personal Element, (as indicated by the Year of birth).

THE DESTRUCTIVE CYCLE

In the destructive cycle:
WOOD destroys(saps) EARTH.
EARTH destroys (absorbs) WATER.
WATER destroys (puts out) FIRE.
FIRE destroys (melts) METAL
METAL destroys (cuts) WOOD.

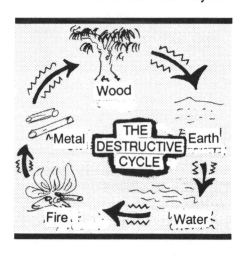

The Destructive Cycle.

Application principles for both negative and positive Cycles of the Elements follow similiar guidelines. While identifying the "good" and "bad" Elements vis-a-vis a person's own governing Element (based on Year of Birth) is not difficult, sometimes weighing the "too much" or "too little" factor can be an onerous exercise. Making this kind of judgement is also subjective.

As pointed out in the previous section, when there is a surfeit of any single Element, it may be necessary to counter the excess with the presence of a destructive Element in the interests of achieving balance in one's individual persona.

For Feng Shui purposes, knowledge of the destructive cycle serves to alert one to "what may be hurtful" within one's environment. For example if a person was born in a FIRE year, then obviously lots of plants (WOOD) in the house must surely be agreeable; while the presence of water (aquariums, ponds, fountains and so forth) is not desirable, since WATER destroys FIRE.

Definately, using the previous example of the businessman's name, "Tua Hai" will be unsuitable, since the "big sea" will completely obliterate the FIRE.

GENERAL APPLICATIONS

In Compass School Feng Shui, the Texts suggest that equally important (and therefore just as significant and potent in its effects) to the Element represented by one's Year of Birth is the Element indicated by the best or most auspicious Lo Shu numbers. In Chapter Three, the Formulations and Tables from which the reader may determine his best Lo-Shu number(s) is presented. The auspicious Lo Shu number corresponds to one of the eight Trigrams, which in turn is symbolised by one of the Elements. Using the Element so identified, one is then able to apply the principles of the Productive or Destructive Cycle to one's advantage.

APPLYING ELEMENT ANALYSES TO THE PA-KUA

The Pa-Kua illustrated here shows the specific Element of each of the Trigrams which have been arranged around the Pa-Kua according to the Later Heaven Arrangement. Each Trigram represents a compass direction based on this Arrangement. Feng Shui practitioners can co-relate (match) each of the Elements to each of the directions and act accordingly.

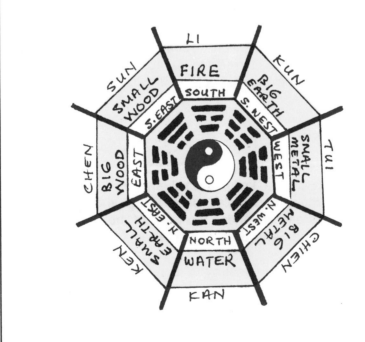

The inter-actions of the Five Elements to each other when examined in relation to the magical connotations of the Pa-Kua, take on deeper and more profound associations. Thus for example, three of the five Elements are indicated as being "big" or "small".

This is shown in the drawing of the Pa-Kua in the previous page.

Thus:
Big WOOD is East (The Trigram Chen)
Small WOOD is S.East (The Trigram Sun)

Big METAL is N.West (The Trigram Chien)
Small METAL is West (The Trigram Tui)

Big EARTH is S.West (The Trigram Kun)
Small EARTH is N.East (The Trigram Ken)

The two opposing Elements FIRE and WATER stand by themselves and are represented as South (The Trigram Li) and North (The Trigram Kan) respectively.

According to the old texts on the Pa-Kua and Lo-Shu Method of Feng Shui analyses, while the productive and destructive cycles of the Elements offer general indications of compatability or hostility between the respective Elements, it is also to be recognised that upon deeper reflection other additional aspects of the relationships are to be appraised.

.THUS CONSIDER:

* While METAL is said to destroy WOOD, it may be argued that a small Metal (an axe, a knife, a saw) shapes the Big Wood into furniture, into chairs and tables, so that now the Metal no longer destroys, but instead enhances the value of the Wood. Surely then small Metal is good Feng Shui for Big Wood ?

* While WATER is said to destroy FIRE, it may be observed that Fire is good for small water, in that it boils the water, turns it into steam and creates energy and power from the steam. Once again two hostile elements can be "good" for each other.

Surely the production of energy must represent good Feng Shui ?

* While EARTH is said to destroy WATER, surely it can be seen that combining Earth and Water produces a fertile environment for the growth of plants and trees, bringing life into the picture. One without the other is of no use. Surely then, small earth and water must be good Feng Shui. It is only the big earth which will absorb the water.

* While WOOD is said to produce FIRE, surely it must be obvious that too much wood can also destroy the fire. Thus surely it is only the small wood that is good Feng Shui for Fire.

* While EARTH is said to produce METAL, this surely must refer only to big earth. How can small earth produce metal ? Thus it is big earth which is good Feng Shui for Metal.

Next, the Texts urge a second look at the Cycles themselves. While the negative and positive cycles offer one single perspective of the Elements, there are also other sub-relationships which must be considered. Thus while WATER destroys FIRE, so can Big EARTH. And FIRE can also destroy WOOD, the way it destroys METAL.

It is further pointed out that only three of the Elements always exist in a tangible form ie METAL, WOOD and EARTH. The remaining two ie FIRE and WATER "disappears". FIRE when it is put out ceases to exist, and WATER "evaporates" into the atmosphere.

The implications of this on Feng Shui, according to the texts is that METAL, WOOD and EARTH cannot be dissolved into nothingness. This aspect of their relationship is used when considering "suitable dates". According to the Chinese Almanac, every single day of the year is represented by one of the five Elements (indicated in Chinese style daily calendars). As such if one's best Lo Shu number is either North or South ie representing WATER or FIRE, it is imperative that when selecting days for important activities, it is vital not to select a day which corresponds to an Element that can destroy FIRE or WATER since these Elements can dissolve into nothing, thus totally destroying your good luck. The other three Elements are not as vulnerable.

One can further interpret other permutations of the relationship between the five Elements. The main determinant to consider is balance. Elements per se draw one picture. When size and magnitude redefine them, the picture changes thus transforming the outcome.

OTHER INTERPRETATIONS

Theories of the Five Elements (Wu Xing) have a long continious history in Chinese civilisation with much of ancient Chinese architecture being influenced by these theories, ie quite apart from the pre-occupation with Feng Shui.

According to Chinese scholars the nature of the Five Elements was first explained in the "Chou Shu" during the period of the sixth century BC, which listed these Elements in order - Water, Fire, Wood, Metal/gold and Earth. These were said to represent the five different kinds of matter which people constantly came in contact with.

But it is the essence of the Elements rather than the Elements themselves which, in combination, cause each other, as well as all other things to occur; in the wrong combination they can be mutually destructive. Combinations of the Elements can cause great happiness or distress to human life as we have seen when we examined the Productive and the Destructive cycles.

But there is more to the Elements than merely their intrinsic nature. Each of the Elements also represent or symbolise other things which suggests further interpretations of their meanings and inter-relationships. The Table here suggest six other "inter-relationships".

	WOOD	FIRE	EARTH	METAL	WATER
direction	east	south	centre	west	north
weather	wind	heat	damp	dry	cold
time of life	birth	growth	develop	maturity	old-age
emotion	anger	happy	reason	love	fear
music note	*jue*	*zhi*	*gong*	*shang*	*yu*
colour	green	red	yellow	white	black

From the Table we perceive all sorts of possible combinations between the five directions, the five colours, the five notes of the musical scale, the five weather/atmospheric elements and the five emotions.

Interpretations of these combinations are primarily guided by the Productive and Destructive cycles, although other factors are also always considered.

Further insights may be gained if we examine in detail one other aspect of the Elements. Take the five colours.

Of these colours, green (or blue) is the colour of sprouting leaves. It symbolises the tenderness of spring, the germination of seedlings, the period of of the beginning, and it corresponds to the East.

Following this analysis, structures located in the Eastern part of the house should ideally be covered with green tiles or be painted green, or perhaps a nursery can be sited there ... this method of applying the theory of the Elements brings about harmony within the environment especially if all other parts of the home are similiarly addressed.

In the Forbidden City in Beijing for instance, buildings which were located on the Eastern part of the City were covered with green glazed tiles. There was another reason for these green tiles. They were used because in the stages of life according to the Five Elements, youth corresponded to Wood and East. These Eastern buildings housed the young princes when the srructures were built during the Chien Lung period of the Ching Dynasty.
Thus the green tiled roofs.

For similiar reasons, because the empress dowager and the concubines of the late emperor were at a mature age then, their stage in life corresponded with that of Metal, the West. For this reason the empress's quarters were situated on the Western wing of the palace complex and the rooms within were painted white.

Within the Forbidden Palace are further examples which demonstrate the use of the five colour aspect of Element relationships. Thus for example in the Palace Altar, terraces were constructed with soils of five different colours according to their respective directions.
The walls surrounding the altar were also covered with different coloured tiles; green in the East, red in the South, white in the West, black in the North and yellow in the Centre !

These details must surely demonstrate the vast influence and belief in this ancient theory.

Within the latter day context, it is not difficult to incorporate theories of the five Elements into the practice of Feng Shui especially when selecting colour schemes for rooms and structures, roof and floor tiles ... Just remember that the five Elements interpret the structure of the Universe and thus, must be viewed as dynamic and interacting rather than as static, unchanging forces.

Recognize also that depending on their proximity to each other, they are mutually destructive or productive.

Such a cyclical view permeates almost all other aspects of Chinese philosophy, no less so in the practice of Feng Shui. For this reason, or perhaps more likely because of it, we must now examine the Book of Changes, or I-Ching to delve deeper into this concept of circular moving forces which lead to dynamic change in the lives of mankind.

CHAPTER TWO

THE I-CHING & THE PA-KUA

THE I-CHING or BOOK OF CHANGES

The seasoned wisdom of thousands of years has gone into the makings of the I-Ching. Both branches of Chinese philosophy- Confucianism and Taoism have their common roots here. And the I-Ching alone, among all the Confucian Classics escaped the great burning of books under the emperor Chin Shih Huang Ti in 213 B.C.

The origins of the I-Ching go back to mythical antiquity. As a Book of Divination or as a Book of Wisdom, the I-Ching has occupied the attention of China's most eminent scholars through the centuries down to the present day.

All that is great and significant in the three thousand years of Chinese cultural history has taken its inspiration from this Book. Not only the philosophy of the Chinese race, but also its science and statecraft have borrowed from the distinctive wisdoms of the I-Ching.

Even the common-places and practice of everyday life in China are saturated with its influence.

It is from this singularly great book that much of the cryptic secrets of Feng Shui has its origins.

Almost all aspects of Feng Shui's multitudinous related principles and symbolisms, its view of the Trinity Heaven, Earth and Man, its dependence on the Pa-Kua, the Lo-Shu Magic Grid, Concepts of Balance and Harmony, Interactions of Yin and Yang, Positive and Negative ... were collectively derived either from interpretations of the

Texts of the I-Ching, or from the roots of the I-Ching itself.

The influence of the I-Ching on Feng Shui philosophy and procedures is most particularly seen in the prominent role played by the Eight sided Pa-Kua symbol, with its Eight Trigrams. Indeed much of the so called "Diviners Formulae" are derived from the special placement and symbolic connotations of these Trigrams, which themselves are also the origins of the I-Ching's 64 Hexagrams.

There is thus a close inter-relationship between various Feng Shui formulae and the I-Ching's divination aspects and this is reflected in similiar philosophical concepts of harmony and balance which both embody.

In view of these similiarities, attempts at differentiating the layers of images and symbols from the layers of concepts that represent the whole body of Feng Shui knowledge, must surely entail examining the classical I-Ching in some depth, primarily its origins and history, as well as the derivatives of its Hexagrams.

Understanding its origin fosters valuable insights into the characteristics and interpretations of the Trigrams of the Pa-Kua.

These Trigrams, as we shall see in Chapter Three when we begin to study Pa-Kua Lo-Shu Feng Shui, play a central role in assisting the Feng Shui practitioner understand what needs to be done to improve his/her Feng Shui.

Knowledge of the Trigrams and its related symbols vastly increase and expand the theoretical basis for many of Feng Shui's so called guidelines. Such understanding must surely lend greater credence to the practise of the geomancer's art.

There are not many authentic or reliable translations of the I-Ching.

The earliest translations were published in the late nineteenth century (undertaken by Western academics de'Harlez and James Legge).

But surely the most comprehensive and finest translation of the I-Ching must be the one undertaken by Richard Wilhelm who spent over ten years working on the Texts and related Commentaries of the I-Ching.

Long residence in China, mastery of both the written and spoken language and close association with the cultural leaders of the day made it possible for him to perceive the Chinese Classics, and grasp its profusion of images from the Chinese perspective.

Wilhelm started work on the project in 1911 after the Chinese revolution, when Tsingtao became the residence of several eminent classical scholars. Among them was Lao Nai-Tsuan, who in the words of Wilhelm in the Preface of his translation "... opened my mind to the wonders of the Book of Changes".

Lao was a scholar of the old school, one of the last of his kind who was thoroughly familiar with the great field of Commentary literature that grew up around the I-Ching through the centuries. Under Lao's experienced guidance and after much detailed discussions, translation of the Text proceeded.

The project was interrupted by the outbreak of the world war but was later resumed and completed. "Those were rare hours of inspiration that I spent with my aged master" says Wilhelm.

Wilhelm's I-Ching was translated into German, and it was left to another scholar Cary F. Baynes to render it into English, thus making the great wisdom of the I-Ching available to a broader audience.

Overseas Chinese like the author and many of her contemporaries whose knowledge of and exposure to so called "authentic Chinese Culture" is at best adapted and juxtaposed from a hodge podge of secondary literature, superstition and hearsay from the old folks; owe a debt of gratitude to both Wilhelm and Baynes for making this great work accessible for study.

For implicit in this particular translation of the I-Ching is the fact that it addresses itself not only to the world of academia, but also, and perhaps more so, to individuals everywhere who are concerned about their inter-action with the forces of Nature, to the Universe and to their fellow men. And to those of us who attempt to push aside the veil that shrouds much of the Chinese metaphysical sciences (including Feng Shui).

A great deal of the research undertaken by the author into the origins and meanings of the I-Ching have been extracted from the Richard

Wilhelm translation, although, where applicable, references have also been made to the James Legge translation as well as to the more recently published "Chinese Coin Divination through the I-Ching" written by Da Lui.

Readers who wish to delve deeper are strongly recommended to try and locate the Wilhelm book.

THE ORIGINS OF THE I-CHING

Four legendary, almost mythical personalities are credited with the authorship and evolution of the I-Ching or Book of Changes. These are Fu Hsi; King Wen, his son, the Duke of Chou and Confucius the most famous of China's great thinkers.

Fu Hsi is said to have invented the linear signs manifested as the eight three lined TRIGRAMs. These first appeared in two major collections, the I-Ching of the mythical Hsia Dynasty (around 2205 B.C.) called *Lien Shan* and the I-Ching of the Shang Dynasty entitled *Kuei Ts'ang*. *These Trigrams are the roots of the Hexagrams which came later, and are also featured as vital components of the Pa-Kua symbol.*

The legendary Fu Hsi.

King Wen, the progenitor of the Chou Dynasty (1150-249 BC) took the Trigrams further and formulated the 64 HEXAGRAMS. These came about by doubling the Trigrams from three line symbols into six line symbols, done in multiple combinations of the Trigrams themselves.

Thus there were 8x8 combinations resulting in 64 permutations. King Wen was also said to have appended brief judgements to each of the Hexagrams, thereupon laying the groundwork for much of the acknowledged wisdom of I-Ching philosophy.

His son, the dynamic Duke of Chou authored the Texts pertaining to each of the individual lines of the Hexagrams, assigning meanings to them as and when they changed.

His contributions were entitled the Changes of Chou and these subsequently came to be used as oracles. These Changes, which are contained in a number of ancient historical records, drastically altered the complexion of the I-Ching, indeed expanding its philosophy to take on colourings of divination.

The great sage CONFUCIUS.

This was the status of the book when the great sage Confucius came upon it. Confucius devoted the best part of his life to studying the Texts, Judgements and images of the I-Ching, and he too expanded the Book's scope with a series of Commentaries generally referred to as the "Wings". A great deal of literature grew up around the book during this period, fragments of which continue to be part of the Commentaries of the modern day I-Ching. These Commentaries, in parts differ greatly in interpretation and content, to the extent that Confucius' role in the evolution of I-Ching philosophy cannot be overstated. His disciples also did further work on the I-Ching.

The Book of Changes escaped the fate of other Classics at the time of the famous burning of books under the tyrant emperor Chin Shih Huang Ti. But by that time the I-Ching had become firmly established as a Book of divination and magic.

It was around this time also, ie the third century BC, that the Yin-Yang doctrine ran riot in connection with popular interpretations of the I-Ching undertaken by the Han Scholars of that period. Their atitudes and inclination tended towards magnifying the mysterious and magical aspects of the I-Ching's contents.

It was not until around 226 AD that the Book of Changes came to be regarded also as a Book of Wisdom, and by the time of the Sung period (960-1279) the book had evolved further, this time as a textbook relating to state-craft and the philosophy of life.

In the thirteenth century, successful attempts were made to revive the I-Ching as a Book of Oracles and this metaphysical view of the Book has continued to the present day.

During the time of the last dynasty of China, interpretations and commentaries of the book once again tended to take inspiration from the Han scholars and were thus much influenced by theories of magic. This view of the I-Ching has since remained and today it is regarded as one of the exalted Divination Texts of China.

During the K'ang Hsi period, a comprehensive version of the Book finally emerged. This separated the Texts from the Commentaries with the latter fully incorporating extracts that had survived the centuries. The Wilhelm translation is based on this Kang Hsi edition.

This brief expose of the path travelled by the I-Ching through the ages offers insights into its content and meanings, especially the profusion of imagery and symbolisms contained in the descriptions and the judgements of the lines of the Hexagrams.

In this connection it is useful to remember that the development of Feng Shui thought and practice, occured alongside that of the Book of Changes, at least from the Tang period onwards, so that even as perspectives of the I-Ching altered from one century to the next, a parallel development also impacted on the practice of, and conceptual approach towards Feng Shui. The significance of this becomes evident when we begin to question the source of Feng Shui's apparent potency. Does it really work ? In like manner one can similiarly question the efficacy of the I-Ching as a Book of Divination. Can it really fore-tell outcomes ?

Both are suggestive of magical connotations. Both are based on similiar styles of imagery particularly the linear symbols called Trigrams and Hexagrams, whose connections to Nature (ie the seasons and landscapes); the forces of Nature (Wind, Water, Fire and Thunder) and to compass directions appear to exhibit unique manifestations of supernatural, or at least metaphysical forces at work. One must admit with some degree of reverence and humility, that surely a practice as complex as Feng Shui, and a wisdom as profound as the I-Ching could only have survived the vagaries of time because its potency which has kept generation after generation enthralled and mesmerised, must truly be genuine.

THE LATER HEAVEN PA-KUA

WITH CORRESPONDING DIRECTIONS, TRIGRAMS AND OTHER SYMBOLISMS SUMMARISED.

The Yin Yang symbol represented in the centre of the Pa-Kua reflect the "Way of Heaven and Earth". This means that everything can be divided into the two mutually opposing and independent elements of Yin and Yang. This follows the belief that all things on earth consist of the unity of opposites. Hence the various symbols depicted within the eight sides of the Pa-Kua and associated with the corresponding Trigrams reflects this dualistic view of the Universe.

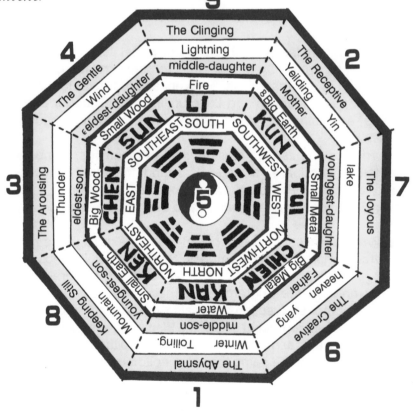

43

THE TRIGRAMS

The eight primary Trigrams are the roots of the I-Ching's 64 Hexagrams. Each Trigram comprise combinations of three straight lines that are either broken (━ ━) or unbroken (━━━).

These Trigrams collectively symbolise and represent a Trinity of world principles that are recognised as the Subject (man), the Object having form (earth) and the Content (heaven). The lowest place in the Trigram is that of Earth; the middle place belongs to Man; and the top place to Heaven.

A globular concept of the Universe is thus deemed to be fully expressed by the aggregate meanings of the eight Trigrams.

Another significant feature of the Trigrams is that they intermingle, and in so doing create new aspects to their relationships. This intermingling is expressed as "Heaven and Earth determining the directions "; as "Mountain and Lake uniting"; as "Thunder and Wind arousing" each other, as "Water and Fire not combating" each other.

Every Trigram has its own multiple sets of meanings, symbols and connotations, and are "arranged" around the eight sides of the octogonal shaped Pa-Kua in two recognised sequences, the Early Heaven Sequence or Arrangement and the Later Heaven Sequence.

Extensive references are frequently made to these Trigrams by Feng Shui practitioners of the Compass School. This is because the meanings of the Trigrams offer valuable "clues" to the practitioner in that, not only do the Trigrams each have corresponding cardinal points and compass directions, they also, in addition to the symbolism mentioned above, represent one of the Elements, expressed either as a soft or a dark aspect and possessing either a yin or yang connotation; and at the same time also epitomize a specific member of the family.

Permutations of these attributes of the Trigrams generally result in multiple interpretations which are not easy to comprehend.

Nevertheless these meanings and interpretations are often significant in that they expand the scope of Feng Shui Practice while simultaneously suggesting clues as to what can be "activated", and how the symbolisms, either singly or collectively, can be interpreted in the physical realm, to bring about auspicious outcomes.

This is especially the case once the specific Trigram(s) deemed "lucky" in accordance to an individual's horoscope has been ascertained.

The method for determining one's "lucky" Trigram(s) is explained in detail in Chapter Three. Basically each individual is considered either a "west" person or an "east" person, and each individual has four "lucky" directions and four "inauspicious" directions.

The crux of Pa-Kua Lo-Shu Feng Shui (sometimes referred to as the 9 star method of Feng Shui) is to first discover what these lucky and unlucky directions are, and then proceed from there. However, before advancing to commence that exercise, it is strongly recommended that as much of the connotations of the Trigrams, and their interactions be fully understood first.

The eight Trigrams are CHIEN the Creative, KUN the Receptive, CHEN the Arousing, SUN the Gentle, TUI the Joyous, KEN, keeping Still, KAN the Abysmal, and LI the Clinging.

These Trigrams, with their major symbolisms and meanings are described here in detail:

THE TRIGRAM "CHIEN", the Creative, *comprise three unbroken lines. Its nature is YANG and it is often associated with the FATHER, the head of the household, the patriarch, the male paternal. Chien also signifies HEAVEN, the sky, the celestial spheres, strength, activity, power, brightness, bright colours, energy and perseverance. Chien doubled, forms the first Hexagram of the I-Ching whose power is to be interpreted in a dual sense ie in terms of the strong creative action of the Diety of the Universe and in terms of the creative action of rulers or leaders in the world of Mankind.*

The Element associated with Chien is big METAL, and its symbolic animal is the HORSE denoting power, endurance, firm-ness and strength.

Additional symbols of the Creative include jade which is itself the symbol of purity and firm-ness (so, likewise is metal), round and circular objects, cold, ice. Its corresponding compass direction is South under the Early Heaven Arrangement of the Pa-Kau, and Northwest under the Later Heaven Arrangement. In the practice of Feng Shui, the Later Arrangement compass direction, ie Northwest is the relevant direction.

THE TRIGRAM "KUN", the Receptive is made up of three broken lines. The broken lines represents the dark, yeilding, receptive, primal power of YIN. The attribute of this Trigram refer to the MOTHER, the female maternal and devotion; and its image is the whole EARTH, which knows no partiality. The animal symbolising Kun is the COW with a calf, thereby symbolising fertility.

Kun is the perfect complement of Chien, the Creative (complement and not opposite because the Receptive does not combat the Creative but rather completes it). Kun signifies NATURE, in contrast to spirit, Earth in contrast to Heaven, Space against Time, the Female Maternal as against the Male Paternal.

In the interpretation of Kun in respect of the destinies of mankind, and when applied to human affairs, the relationship between Chien and Kun refers not only to the man-woman relationship but also to that of the prince and the minister, the father and the son, employer and employee.

According to the I-Ching's commentary, Kun the Receptive must be activated and led by Chien the Creative if it is to maximise its production of good. The corresponding compass direction of Kun is North in the Early Heaven Arrangement and SOUTH-WEST in the Later Heaven Arrangement.

THE TRIGRAM "CHEN", the Arousing is made up of two broken Yin lines above an unbroken Yang line. The Trigram represents the ELDEST SON, and is often associated with movement and decision making, vehemence and shock. Its image is THUNDER, and it is symbolised by the DRAGON, which, rising out from the depths, soars magnificently up to the stormy skies. This is represented by the single strong line pushing upward below the two yeilding lines. This Trigram is represented by dark yellow colour, spreading outwards, which suggests the luxuriant growth of Spring that covers the

Earth with a garment of plants. Thus the Element of this Trigram is big WOOD. In the I-Ching, the doubling of this Trigram forms the Hexagram Chen, which is described as "...shock, arousing fear, which in turn makes one cautious, and caution brings good fortune ... a symbol of inner calm in the midst of the storm of outer movement."

Kun also signifies thunder, "the kind which terrifies for miles around, a symbol of a mighty ruler who knows how to make himself respected yet is careful and exact in the smallest detail". Chen is placed North-East in the Early Heaven Arrangement and represents EAST in the Later Heaven Sequence.

THE TRIGRAM "SUN", the Gentle, is formed by two unbroken yang lines above a broken yin line. This Trigram represents the ELDEST DAUGHTER and its attribute is summed up in the word "penetrating". The gentle is small WOOD, it is the wind, it is indecision. It is symbolised by the COCK whose voice pierces the still morning air. Among men, it means those with broad foreheads, those with much white in their eyes; it means those close to making gains, so that in the market they get threefold value. Sun is sometimes interpreted as a sign of vehemence. Sun also represents white and whiteness, which is sometimes regarded as the colour of the yin principle. Here yin is in the lowest place at the beginning. Sun is placed South-West in the Early Heaven Arrangement and in SOUTH-EAST in the Later Heaven Arrangement.

THE TRIGRAM TUI, the Joyous comprise one broken yin line above two unbroken yang lines. The two yang lines are considered the rulers of the Trigram although they are inacapable of acting as governing rulers. Tui represents joy, happiness and the YOUNGEST DAUGHTER. Tui is the Element small METAL. It is also the LAKE, which rejoices and refreshes all living things.

Futhermore Tui is the mouth; when human beings give joy to one another through their feelings it is manifested by the mouth. A yin line becomes manifest above two yang lines;

this shows how the two principles give joy to each other and is manifested outwardly. Tui also means dropping off and bursting open. Among kinds of soil it is hard and salty. It is the concubine, an association derived from the youngest daughter connections. It is the sheep, which is outwardly weak and inwardly stubborn, as suggested by the form of the Trigram.

Under the Former Heaven Arrangement, the Trigram is placed South-east, but in the Later Heaven Arrangement it stands in the WEST, and is therefore connected with the idea of AUTUMN. Most important of all for Feng Shui practice is to remember that Tui symbolises pleasure.

THE TRIGRAM KEN,

Keeping Still, comprises an unbroken yang line above two broken yin lines. Ken represents the YOUNGEST SON in the family. The Trigram literally means standing still, a situation exemplified by the image of the mountain.
This symbol of the mountain is of mysterious significance. Here, in the deep hidden stillness, the end of everything is joined to make a new beginning.

Death and life, dying and resurrection - these are thoughts awakened by the transition from an old year to a new year. Ken thus signifies a time of solitude which is also the link between an ending and a beginning. The Element signified by Ken is small EARTH; and under the Former Heaven Sequence of the Trigrams, it is placed in the North-west. Under the Later Heaven Arrangement Ken is NORTHEAST.

THE TRIGRAM KAN,

... the Abysmal is made up of one unbroken yang line sandwiched between two broken yin lines. Kan represents the MIDDLE SON. Its Element is WATER, and its season is WINTER. Kan signifies pearl, craftiness and hidden things. It is also considered as a symbol of Danger and Melancholia because one (strong) yang line is hemmed in by two (weak) yin lines. Kan is often referred to as the Trigram which suggests "toil". Unlike the other Trigrams, Kan represents work. It is not a happy Trigram.

The symbolic colour of Kan is red, ie the red that resembles the fluid of the body ie blood. Kan was originally placed West in the Early Heaven Arrangement, but was moved to the North under the Later Heaven Arrangement, the place formerly occupied by Kun, the Receptive.

Finally THE TRIGRAM LI,

... the Clinging, made up of one broken line in the centre hemmed in by two strong yang lines. Li is FIRE, and represents the MIDDLE DAUGHTER. Li is also the sun, brightness, lightning, heat and dryness. The character of the Trigram suggests something firm on the outside but hollow, weak and yeilding within.

This Trigram strongly implies dependence, but the kind of dependence which is positive and nourishing, as when the plant "clings" to the soil and grows or when "the sun and the moon attain their brightness by clinging to heaven". The yeilding element in Li is the central line, hence its image is of a strong yet docile type of cow.

More, fire flames upwards, hence the phrase "...that which is bright rises". In the spiritual or divination sense, the brightness of this Trigram offers the potential (if the illumination of the brightness stays consistent) for   its light to "illuminate" the world.

Also while Li occupies the East in the Early Heaven Arrangement its place under the Later Heaven Arrangement is the SOUTH which represents the summer sun that illuminates all earthly things.

In the Book of Changes there are additional symbols connected to the Trigrams, as well as extensive Commentaries which offer critiques on the character of the lines themselves.

For purposes of Feng Shui however, the significant aspects of the Trigrams relate mainly (although not exclusively) to their directions, their Elements, the member of the family they represent and the basic features of Nature which each embody.

Understanding these principal connections is normally sufficient to understanding the fundamental derivatives of much of Feng Shui practice and methodologies.

THE SEQUENTIAL ARRANGEMENTS

Of somewhat added significance to enhancing one's knowledge of Compass School Feng Shui is a sensitive appreciation of the sequential arrangements of the Trigrams, arrangements which characterise the origins of the Pa-Kua and also expresses the "view" of Man's existence through the Pa-Kua. According to Tradition there are two accepted Arrangements, the Early Heaven and the Later Heaven.

THE EARLY HEAVEN ARRANGEMENT

Here the eight Trigrams are named in a sequence of pairs which, according to folklore, goes back to the original founder, Fu Hsi, and was thus already in existence by the time of the Chou Dynasty. This Early Sequence formation, also known as the Primal Arrangement places the two Trigrams Chien and Kun, the Creative and the Receptive, the Heaven and the Earth, in the South and North positions respectively. These two totally Yang and totally Yin Trigrams thus determined the North-South axis.

Then follows the Ken-Tui axis, ie the Mountain and the Lake; their forces inter-related, in that the wind blows from the mountain to the lake while clouds and the mists rise from the lake to the mountain. The relationship suggested is thus circular. The Ken-Tui axis are represented by the directions North-West and South-East.

The third axis is formed by Chen and Sun, ie Thunder and Wind which strenghthen each other whenever they emerge. This is positioned North-East and South-West.

Finally the Trigrams Li and Kan which is Fire and Water make up the concluding axis. Though these two elements appear at first to be irreconcilable opposites in the physical world, according to Fu Hsi, in their Primal, or "original" state they balance each other so that there is in reality, no conflict between them at all !
This view of Water and Fire must be given due consideration when analysing the inter-relationships of the Five Elements especially considering that under the conventional Destructive Cycle, Water is described as "destroying Fire."

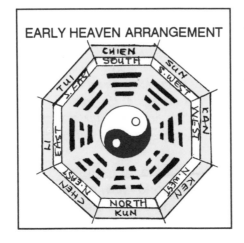

EARLY HEAVEN ARRANGEMENT

It is further suggested that when the Trigrams begin to move and intermingle, a double movement can be observed:

first, the usual clockwise movement which is cumulative and expanding forward, moving and ascending, so that as time progresses, this forward movement determines the events which come to pass;

second, there is also an opposite backward motion, which folds and contracts, even as time passes, thereby creating "seeds" for the future. The explanation is that if the essence of this backward movement is understood, then the situation of the future unfolds clearly ...

The Primal Arrangement also express the forces of Nature in terms of "pairs of opposites". Thus, Thunder, an electrically charged force has Wind as its opposite. The Rain, which moistens the seeds and enables it to germinate, has the Sun, which supplies warmth, as its opposite. This example further demonstrates the contention that "water and fire do not combat each other".

In comprehending opposite moving forces, consider the Trigram Ken, Keeping Still whose situation describes the termination of any extra expansion and growth. Its "opposite", the Joyous brings forth "the harvest". Consider also the directing forces of the Creative and the Receptive, which together represent the great laws of existence; these two also comprise a pairing of opposites....

The above expositions of the Primal Arrangement seem to suggest ascending and descending forces.
Understanding these forces supposedly reveals the "secrets of the future" because the Primal Arrangement is supposed to express Heaven's view of existence.

Such understanding however, was and is frequently beyond the modest faculties of the human mind. One can only be seduced by the beauty of the imagery even as the full import of their inter-relationships escape us.

51

Thus, Consider this passage:

.... " *God comes forth in the sign of the Arousing (CHEN), he brings all things to completion in the sign of the Gentle (SUN); he causes creatures to perceive one another in the sign of the Clinging (LI); he causes them to serve one another in the sign of the Receptive (KUN), he gives then joy in the sign of the Joyous (TUI); he does battle in the sign of the Creative (CHIEN); he toils in the sign of the Abysmal (KAN); he brings them to perfection in the sign of Keeping Still (KEN).*"

Fortunately, after Fu Hsi came King Wen, who re-formulated the sequence of the Trigrams to offer an "Inner world" view of mankind, a view which seems to take a less profound judgment of the Trigrams.

Thus came about the Later Heaven Arrangement of the Trigrams which definately bears closer resemblance to the Earthly aspects and relationships of the various characteristics of the Trigrams.

According to modern interpretations of the two Arrangements, the Early Heaven Sequence represents the ideal version of the Universe as depicted by the Trigrams, while the Later Heaven Sequence represents the practical application of the Trigrams to the Earth. By extension therefore, the Later Heaven version is supposed to allow for a more strategic and comprehensive view of Man's existence.

The two arrangements also have their equivalent "Hou-Tu" and "Lo-Shu" diagrams, which embellished the "magical" aspects of the Trigrams, but more of this later. At this stage it is necessary and relevant to first examine the Later Heaven Arrangement.

THE LATER HEAVEN ARRANGEMENT

The Later Heaven Arrangement of the Trigrams is also known as the "Inner World" Arrangement. Here the Trigrams are taken out of their groupings in pairs of opposites and instead are shown in a circular temporal progression of their manifestations within the physical earthly realm. What are perceived then are the Cycles of the year with the distinct four seasons, the cycles of each day with its day and night and so forth... Under the new Arrangement therefore, the cardinal points and the seasons seem to be more directly related.

The arrangement of the Trigrams around the Pa-Kua is thus very drastically changed.

THE LATER HEAVEN

Thus consider this extract:

" ... *the year shows the creative activity of God in the Trigram CHEN, the Arousing, which stands in the East and signifies Spring (the beginning) ... All living things come forth in the sign of the Arousing ... They come to completion in the sign of the gentle (SUN) which stands in the South-east. Completeion means that all creatures beome pure and perfect ... the Clinging (LI) is the brightness in which all creatures perceive one another. It is the Trigram of the South. Thus the sages turned to the South (ie the light) whenever they gave ear to the meaning of the Universe ... next comes the Receptive, which means the Earth. The Earth takes care that all creatures are nourished ... TUI or Joyous comes in mid autumn, followed by CHIEN the Creative in the Northwest, and KAN, the Water in the North. Here in this sign of the Abysmal all creatures work ... followed then by the sign of the KEN, Keeping Still, in the Northeast where the beginning and the end find completeion ... thus is the cycle ended ......*"

The sequence of the Trigrams reflects the harmony and intrinsic balance of the year. What is illustrated in the above description is a narration of life as experienced by Nature.

The Trigrams are allotted to the seasons and to the cardinal points to reflect the innate harmony of Nature. One can also extend the annual cycle depicted to that of an ordinary day, such that for instance the Trigram CHEN while signifying Spring, can also be representative of morning, the start of the day.

The next Trigram, SUN represents the wind which melts the ice of winter, and wood which germinates and grows. Which takes us to LI, which is midsummer or noon time (of the day). And so on....with the remaining Trigrams showing the way round the cycle, all the while stressing harmony and balance.

The Later Heaven Arrangement is also more easily understood, its basic premise being closer to the attributes of life on Earth. In view of this, most latter day practice of Chinese Astrology or Feng Shui adopt this sequential representation of the Pa-Kua.

Much of the Ganzhi system of Heavenly Stems and Earthly Branches also co-relate to the Later Heaven Arrangement of the Pa-Kua, as also, do much of Compass Feng Shui Schools. For this reason, most Feng Shui Luo-Pans, though not all, also follow this Arrangement.

It is necessary to make the distinction between the two Arrangements, not only because of the intrinsic differences in philosophies expressed, but also because, from a more practical standpoint, the directions represented by each Trigram are different under the two arrangements.

In the application of Compass Feng Shui methodologies there is a further development which the student practitioner must understand and this is the historically acknowledged fact relating to the "discovery" of the magic grids, the Hou-Tu and the Lo-Shu diagrams.

Much of the discourses on these two diagrams were expounded during the time of the Han Dynasty when scholars of that period focused a great deal on the "magical" and divinitive aspects of both the Pa-Kua and the I-Ching.

Not a great deal of their work has survived the centuries particularly as they relate to "Tao magic".

What seems to have survived have been the ideas relating to the emergence of Yin/Yang theories which focus the spotlight on concepts of balance, while concentrating on the virtues of harmony in the natural environment.

Thus was the Pa-Kua embraced as an active philosophy as opposed to being a fatalistic passive one.

Underlying all the exhortations of "magic" were undercurrents of a profound conviction; and those who actively pursued the wisdom of the Pa-Kua, and its Trigrams, held on to the inevitable conclusion that Destiny can indeed be changed, provided one knew the laws of Destiny and are able to unlock the secrets and the original mechanisms of the Pa-Kua.

The practice of Feng Shui reflects a major aspect of the Chinese pre-occupation with this belief. Indeed Feng Shui seems to be the practice which seems to have survived fairly intact into the twentieth century.

THE LO-SHU MAGIC SQUARE

In attempting to unlock the secrets of the Pa-Kua, ancient and latter day scholars focused on the mysterious Lo-Shu grid or magic square.

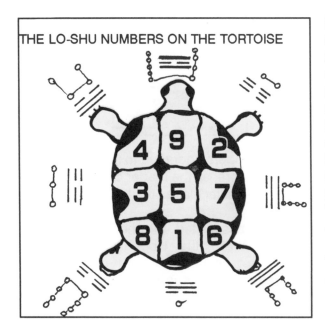

THE LO-SHU NUMBERS ON THE TORTOISE

It is believed that at or around the year 2205 BC (about 4000 years ago), a noble Tortoise emerged from the legendary Lo River, carrying on its huge back, nine numbers that were arranged in a grid pattern. The pattern corresponded to the Pa-Kua's eight Trigrams around a ninth central point.

The numbers were arranged in such a way that adding them up in whatever direction along any three points in a straight line (whether horizontally, vertically or diagonally) added up to the same number ie 15, which coincides with the number of days in each of the 24 phases of the Solar year.

The arrangement of the numbers into a 3 by 3 nine chamber grid came to exert a powerful and mythical influence on Chinese cultural symbolism. The pattern of numbers soon became irretrievably connected with the Trigrams of the Later Heaven Pa-Kua.

At the same time, symbolisms extended connections between the numbers and the Four Celestial Animals (the Dragon, the Tortoise, the Tiger and the Phoenix) as well as with the Five Elements. The Lo-Shu Grid also became the foundation of Taoist magical practice, and many of Taoism's Rituals continue to be synchronised in accordance with the Lo-Shu pattern.

The Lo-Shu was by no means the first pattern of numbers. 900 years earlier, around 2943 BC, Chinese myths claim that Fu Hsi himself had received a formation of numbers, which, according to legend, was brought to him on the back of a dragon horse that emerged out of the Yellow River ! This particular pattern of numbers, referred to as the Hou-Tu Pattern of numbers, (shown in the diagram here) were arranged

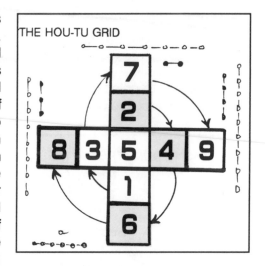

THE HOU-TU GRID

such that all the odd, or even numbers added up to 20 if one ignored the central number 5. (and therefore, as the reader can see the Hou-Tu pattern is no-where near as spectacular as the Lo-Shu pattern !).

The Hou-Tu diagram is usually associated with the Trigrams of the Early Heaven Arrangement. While the Hou-Tu's existence is acknowledged, there does not seem to be the same level of excitement regarding the potency of its qualities compared to what has been attributed to the Lo-Shu. The mystical and mysterious attributes of the Lo-Shu Grid have occupied both religious and philosophical scholars through the ages and it survives today as an acknowledged mystery, still potent, and still guarding its secrets.

So called Lo-Shu "magic" features strongly in Compass School methods of Feng Shui. Old masters perceive in the square, extremely close connections with the trigrams arranged in the Later Heaven Sequence.

The Feng Shui formula and practice described in this book (Chapter Three) and around which some of today's Compass School takes inspiration from is closely allied to the mysterious secrets of the Lo-Shu Grid.

Scholars who have attempted to study the origins of the Lo-Shu Grid speculate that there are striking similiarities between the Grid's numbers and certain potent symbols from other cultures, in particular the ancient Hebrew Cultures whose reputedly powerful Saturnic sign, the "Sigil of the planet Saturn" is similiar in some respects to the Lo Shu. While much of such study must remain speculation considering we are attempting to understand a very complex formula whose origins go back to antiquity, the irrefutable fact remains that there appears to exist a body of knowledge within the Chinese Cultural psyche, (whose origins may or may not have been allied with those of other cultures) which seems to demonstrate important clues regarding the true workings of the forces of the Universe.

"It is a curious fact," writes the eminent psychologist C.G Jung, "that such a gifted and intelligent people as the Chinese has never developed what we call science..".

Jung traces this perception to the western approach to science. He says Western science is predicated on causality, which is regarded as an axiomatic truth. But these same axioms of causality are being shaken to their foundations today: we know now, that what we term scientific laws are "merely statistical truths which must necessarily allow for exceptions". How does one demonstrate the invariable validity of natural or scientific law ?

Which is surely what so called Feng Shui or Chinese landscape "magic" is all about !!

The practice of a Natural law that is based on the wisdom (science) of ancients: hence the Chinese absorbtion and pre-occupation with harmony and balance, the immutable conviction that in all of Nature there is a force or forces which can be "tapped" to bring forth a more perfect existence. Perhaps this force is the CHi ? The magnificent Dragon's breath whose lyrical name embellishes its phenomenal powers ? Meanwhile, what about the negative and the positive, the complementarity of opposites, a state of existence so eloquently yet cryptically embodied in the Yin Yang philosophy ?

The Lo-Shu magic grid seems to be pointing the way to unravelling some of the secret wisdom of the ancients. Why ? Because the practice of something like Feng Shui which embodies the Lo-Shu does work; it does reward the practitioner with abundant earthly good fortune. Perhaps then, more so than the Pa-Kua it is the Lo-Shu grid with its simple arrangement of numbers, which holds the real key to the wisdom of the ancients; a wisdom so scientific, it could even be termed magic !

PART TWO

COMPASS SCHOOL FORMULA

CHAPTER THREE

PA-KUA LO-SHU FENG SHUI

The Pa-Kua Lo-Shu method of Feng Shui is a personalised technique that is based on the horoscope of the practitioner. Using a series of pre-formulated tables which are presented in the following pages, readers may locate two important sets of information that will enable them to orientate their homes, rooms and offices in a way which creates favourable Feng Shui for them.

The Lo-Shu numbers

These two sets of information are:
a) the four best and four worst directions and
b) the four best and four worst locations within a dwelling place.

It is important to stress the difference here between *directions* and *locations,* since understanding this fundamental difference will greatly assist in preventing mistakes from being made during the vital application stage.

The formula(e) contained in the Pa-Kua Lo-Shu method of Feng Shui orientation represents an important branch of the Hokkien Compass School of Feng Shui.

Most of the books on Feng Shui written in English make little or no reference to this method, and where they do, the allusions are descriptive rather than explanantory or practical. Certainly there is little guidance on the application aspects. It is not possible to determine one's best and worst directions, for example, without having access to the pre-formulated tables (which takes the personal horoscope into account). Neither is it possible to use the so called auspicious directions (or avoid the pernicious ones !) unless one is armed with very detailed instructions and guidelines on usage. An appreciation of the underlying Pa-Kua and Lo-Shu philosophies do not hurt either !

The tables and applications presented in this book are extracted from an antique manual belonging to Master Yap, who came into posession of the handwritten treatise some thirty years ago. The Manual, now tattered and weathered with age had apparently been hand copied from a volume originally written during the Chien Lung period of the Chin Dynasty, by a Feng Shui practitioner in Southern China. A copy of this handwritten original made its way to Malaysia during the early part of this century.

It took Master Yap some three years to break the secrets of the formula and guidelines contained in the Manual. Once understood however, he made extensive practice of the Feng Shui methodologies laid out in the book. In his many years experience with the Manual's guidelines, Master Yap has never seen the Method fail in dramatically improving the lives of his clients and friends. Indeed, not a small number of local business tycoons and millionaires have directly benefited from this Manual.

Many families have also successfully overcome specific problems relating to family, careers, marriage, health and children, after re-orienting their homes or rooms to suit their better or best directions as specified in the Pa-Kua and Lo-Shu Grid.

The author is herself a grateful beneficiary of Master Yap's Pa-Kua Lo-Shu compass direction Feng Shui over the past twenty years.

In employing this method, the recommended way to proceed is to start by familiarising one-self with some knowledge of the origins, characteristics and fundamentals of the PA-KUA (especially the Later Heaven Arrangement Pa-Kua) and its eight Trigrams in order to gain some background understanding of the important symbols, compass directions and elements that make up the components of these Trigrams. It is also necessary to comprehend the origins of the Lo Shu magic square whose arrangement of the nine numbers in its nine chambers are directly related to the Later Heaven Pa Kua. This relationship forms the cornerstone of this method of Feng Shui.

Appreciating the interconnections of the symbols therefore contribute immensely to the method's correct interpretation and practice.

Equally important is a full and in depth understanding of the Five Elements (Fire, Water, Metal, Earth & Wood), how they work in relation to each other, and the many, often complicated influences and effects they have on each other.

In this context one needs to delve deeper and go beyond the simple productive and destructive cycles of the Elements, and also differentiate between for instance, "small wood" and "big wood";

The fundamental concepts referred to here have been treated in considerable depth and commentary in the earlier parts of this book, and readers are strongly counseled to gain at least an appreciation of the inter relationships and importance of symbolisms before proceeding to practise Pa-Kua Lo-Shu Feng Shui.

Finally, the practise of Compass School Feng Shui must never ignore the various components of Form School Feng Shui.

This refers to the landscape and terrain of the environment; to the harnessing of the vital dragon's breath, the Chi flows of the surroundings, concepts of harmony and balance, and most important, the awareness of, and being alert to the presence of "poison arrows" (or Sha Chi).

The natural contours of the land can never be ignored. Nor can the effect of man made structures and sharp edges which could create Sha Chi, the pernicious breath that brings bad luck and misfortune. Almost all Feng Shui Masters and Classical texts are in agreement that such structures are to be avoided or deflected at all costs. Thus even if one's directions are at their best orientations, supposedly in the position to generate massive and abundant good luck, the presence of a deadly poison arrow will completely destroy the good Feng Shui !

Readers who want a comprehensive coverage of Form School Feng Shui which stress Green Dragon, White Tiger landscape configurations please refer to the author's introductory first book on "Feng Shui". The practice of the Pa-Kua Lo-Shu method is part of Compass Feng Shui, and for best results, applications of the suggested uses contained in this book should best be in conjunction with the concepts of landscape (or Form school) Feng Shui.

TABLE 1A: KUA NUMBER for MALES & FEMALES

(LUNAR CALENDAR: 1900 to 1924)

Animal	Exact Year of Birth	Males	Females
Rat (M)	31.1.1900 - 18.2.1901	1	5
Ox (M)	19.2.1901 - 7.2.1902	9	6
Tiger (W)	8.2.1902 - 28.1.1903	8	7
Rabbit (W)	29.1.1903 - 15.2.1904	7	8
Dragon (w)	16.2.1904 - 3.2.1905	6	9
Snake (w)	4.2.1905 - 24.1.1906	5	1
Horse (F)	25.1.1906 - 12.2.1907	4	2
Sheep (F)	13.2.1907 - 1.1.1908	3	3
Monkey(E)	2.1.1908 - 21.1.1909	2	4
Rooster(E)	22.1.1909 - 9.1.1910	1	5
Dog (M)	10.2.1910 - 29.1.1911	9	6
Boar (M)	30.1.1911 - 17.2.1912	8	7
Rat (W)	18.2.1912 - 5.2.1913	7	8
Ox (W)	6.2.1913 - 25.1.1914	6	9
Tiger (w)	26.1.1914 - 13.2.1915	5	1
Rabbit (w)	14.2.1915 - 2.2.1916	4	2
Dragon (F)	3.2.1916 - 22.1.1917	3	3
Snake (F)	23.1.1917 - 10.2 1918	2	4
Horse (E)	11.2 1918 - 31.1.1919	1	5
Sheep (E)	1.2.1919 - 19.2. 1920	9	6
Monkey (M)	20.2.1920 - 7.2 1921	8	7
Rooster (M)	8.2.1921 - 27.1.1922	7	8
Dog (W)	28.1.1922 - 15.2.1923	6	9
Boar (W)	16.2.1923 - 4.2.1924	5	1

THE ELEMENTS: M = Metal; W = Water; w = Wood; F = Fire; E = Earth.

YOUR "KUA" NUMBER

The method for ascertaining auspicious Feng Shui directions and placements according to "Compass Direction Feng Shui" is presented in the following pages.

First, determine your "KUA" (as in Pa Kua) number from your horoscope. This KUA number is based on the horoscope, and is determined according to your Year of Birth using the Lunar calendar. Table 1 which stretches over four pages gives the Kua Numbers for those born from the years 1900 to 1996 for males and females.

The first step therefore is to locate your KUA number from Table 1. To countercheck that the number obtained is correct, it is advisable to check the Animal that coincides with your year of birth. The KUA numbers allocated to the years in the tables were conceived and presented according to mathematical formulae given in the classical texts. The numbers rotate in clockwise and counter clockwise fashion for males and females, so that in most years, males and females have different KUA numbers.

The KUA number is highly significant. From it one derives one's all important Lo Shu numbers. But the KUA number is also indicative of several characteristics which can be utilised in the practice of Feng Shui, for example in determining compatabilities with partners, spouses and children and in identifying immediately the compass directions which are good or bad, suitable or unsuitable.

YOUR LO-SHU NUMBERS

Using your KUA number, the next step is to determine your LO SHU Numbers. These reveal your best and worst locations within the Lo Shu Grid; it is in the knowledgeable or ignorant positioning and interplay of room arrangements according to one's Lo Shu Grid which creates good or bad Feng Shui. For this reason, it is vital to examine the auspicious and the bad Lo Shu numbers closely, carefully understanding the characteristics of each of these numbers in order to maximise their effectiveness in the application stages.

TABLE 1B: KUA NUMBER FOR MALES & FEMALES

(LUNAR CALENDAR 1924 to 1948)

Animal	Exact Year of Birth	Males	Females
Rat (w)	5.2.1924 - 24.1.1925	4	2
Ox (w)	25.1.1925 - 12.1.1926	3	3
Tiger (F)	13.1.1926 - 1.2.1927	2	4
Rabbit (F)	2.2.1927 - 22.1.1928	1	5
Dragon (E)	23.1.1928 - 9.2.1929	9	6
Snake (E)	10.2.1929 - 29.1 1930	8	7
Horse (M)	30.1.1930 - 16.2 1931	7	8
Sheep (M)	17.2.1931 - 5.2.1932	6	9
Monkey(W)	6.2.1932 - 25.1.1933	5	1
Rooster(W)	26.1.1933 - 13.1.1934	4	2
Dog (w)	14.1.1934 - 3.2. 1935	3	3
Boar (w)	4.2.1935 - 23.1.1936	2	4
Rat (F)	24.1.1936 - 10.2.1937	1	5
Ox (F)	11.2.1937 - 30.1.1938	9	6
Tiger (E)	31.1.1938 - 18.2.1939	8	7
Rabbit (E)	19.2.1939 - 7.2.1940	7	8
Dragon (M)	8.2.1940 - 26.1.1941	6	9
Snake (M)	27.1.1941 - 14.2.1942	5	1
Horse (W)	15.2.1943 - 4.2.1943	4	2
Sheep (w)	5.2.1943 - 24.1.1944	3	3
Monkey (w)	25.1.1944 - 12.1.1945	2	4
Rooster (w)	13.1.45 - 1.2.1946	1	5
Dog (F)	2.2.1946 - 21.1.1947	9	6
Boar (F)	22.1.1947 - 9. 2.1948	8	7

THE ELEMENTS: M = Metal; W = Water; w = Wood; F = Fire; E = Earth

TABLE 1C: KUA NUMBER FOR MALES & FEMALES

LUNAR CALENDAR 1948 to 1972)

Animal	Exact Year of Birth	Males	Females
Rat (E)	10.2.1948 - 28.1.1949	7	8
Ox (E)	29.1.1949 - 16.2.1950	6	9
Tiger (M)	17.2.1950 - 5.2.1951	5	1
Rabbit (M)	6.2.1951 - 26.1.1952	4	2
Dragon (W)	27.1.1952 - 13.1.1953	3	3
Snake (W)	14.1.1953 - 2.2.1954	2	4
Horse (w)	3.2.1954 - 23.1.1955	1	5
Sheep (w)	24.1.1955 - 11.1.1956	9	6
Monkey (F)	12.1.1956 - 30.1.1957	8	7
Rooster (F)	31.1.1957 - 17.2.1958	7	8
Dog (E)	18.2.1958 - 7.2.1959	6	9
Boar (E)	8.2.1959 - 27.1.1960	5	1
Rat (M)	28.1.1960 - 14.2.1961	4	2
Ox (M)	15.2. 1961 - 4.2.1962	3	3
Tiger (W)	5.2.1962 - 24.1.1963	2	4
Rabbit (W)	25.1.1963 - 12.2.1964	1	5
Dragon (w)	1.2.1964 - 1.2.1965	9	6
Snake (w)	2.2.1965 - 20.1.1966	8	7
Horse (F)	21.1.1966 - 8.2.1967	7	8
Sheep (F)	9.2.1967 - 29.1.1968	6	9
Monkey (E)	30.1.1968 - 16.2.1969	5	1
Rooster (E)	17.2.1969 - 5.2.1970	4	2
Dog (M)	6.2.1970 - 26.1.1971	3	3
Boar (M)	27.1.1971 - 15.1.1972	2	4

THE ELEMENTS: M = Metal; W = Water; w = Wood; F = Fire; E = Earth

TABLE 1D: KUA NUMBER FOR MALES & FEMALES

LUNAR CALENDAR 1972 to 1996)

Animal	Exact Year of Birth	Males	Females
Rat (W)	16.1.1972 - 2.1.1973	1	5
Ox (W)	3.1.1973 - 22.1.1974	9	6
Tiger (w)	23.1.1974 - 10.2. 1975	8	7
Rabbit (w)	11.2 1975 - 30.1.1976	7	8
Dragon (F)	31.1.1976 - 17.2.1977	6	9
Snake (F)	18.2.1977 - 6.2. 1978	5	1
Horse (E)	7.2. 1978 - 27.1.1979	4	2
Sheep(E)	28.1.1979 - 15.2.1980	3	3
Monkey (M)	16.2.1980 - 4.2. 1981	2	4
Rooster (M)	5.2.1981 - 24.1.1982	1	5
Dog (W)	25.1.1982 - 12.2.1983	9	6
Boar (W)	13.2.1983 - 1.2.1984	8	7
Rat (w)	2.2. 1984 - 19.2.1985	7	8
Ox (w)	20.2.1985 - 8.2 1986	6	9
Tiger (F)	9.2.1986 - 28.1.1987	5	1
Rabbit (F)	29.1.1987 - 16.2.1988	4	2
Dragon (E)	17.2.1988 - 5.2.1989	3	3
Snake (E)	6.2.1989 - 26.1.1990	2	4
Horse (M)	27.1.1990 - 14.2.1991	1	5
Sheep (M)	15.2. 1991 - 3.2.1992	9	6
Monkey(W)	4.2.1992 - 22.1.1993	8	7
Rooster(W)	23.1.1993 - 9.2.1994	7	8
Dog (w)	10.2.1994 - 30.1.1995	6	9
Boar (w)	.31.1.1995 - 18.2.1996	5	1

THE ELEMENTS: M = Metal; W = Water; w = Wood; F = Fire; E = Earth

Starting with the four favourable good luck locations, consult Table 2 (2A or 2B depending on whether you are male of female) to obtain the four Lo Shu numbers that pinpoint your four best locations.

These locations correspond to the square sectors in the Lo Shu Grid, and when superimposed onto your building or house layout, they are the sectors or corners of a house or building which best serves to create good luck for you.

EXAMPLE ONE: If your Date of Birth was the 3rd March 1965 (a Wood Snake), and you are Female, your KUA number is 7. From Table 2B you will note that your good Lo Shu numbers (and therefore your best locations) are 6, 2, 8, and 7 in the Lo-Shu Grid.

EXAMPLE TWO: If you are Male and your date of birth was 28th June 1933 (a Water Rooster) your KUA number is 4, and your lucky locations, as shown in Table 2A, are 1, 9, 3 and 4 in the Grid.

YOUR AUSPICIOUS LOCATIONS

Each of the four excellent "locations" bring slightly different kinds of auspicious "luck". Thus while we have categorised them according to very best, second best and so forth, this distinction is purely for convenience. In actual fact all four locations are excellent. These four locations are described in the Feng Shui Manual as follows:

 1. The Very Best Lo Shu number is SHENG CHI translated to mean "generating breath". This number indicates the location and direction in the Lo Shu Grid which will assist you in getting your timing right. It also brings a great deal of money luck and indeed, it is the location to concentrate on if money is what you wish to have since orientating your Feng Shui according to this location will make you a very prosperous man. Thus after you have found out your Sheng Chi location (and direction) make a point of always remembering it. If you are in politics this location in the Lo Shu will attract a high and honourable position for you. It is also the location which will enable you to have five sons. The Sheng Chi location in the Grid also reveals to you the best corner of your house to site your bedroom and your study. It also identifies your best compass direction, the one which should determine the direction of your main doors.

TABLE 2A: BEST LO SHU NUMBERS FOR MALES

KUA Number	BEST Lo Shu No. (Sheng Chi)	2nd BEST Lo Shu No. (Tien Yi)	3rd BEST Lo Shu No. (Nien Yen)	4th BEST Lo Shu No. (Fu Wei)
1	4	3	9	1
3	9	1	4	3
4	1	9	3	4
9	3	4	1	9
5	8	7	6	2
2	8	7	6	2
6	7	8	2	6
7	6	2	8	7
8	2	6	7	8

TABLE 2B: BEST LO SHU NUMBERS FOR FEMALES

KUA NUMBER	BEST Lo Shu No. (Sheng Chi)	2nd BEST Lo Shu No. (Tien Yi)	3rd BEST Lo Shu No. (Nien Yen)	4TH BEST Lo Shu No. (Fu Wei)
1	4	3	9	1
3	9	1	4	3
4	1	9	3	4
9	3	4	1	9
5	2	6	7	8
2	8	7	6	2
6	7	8	2	6
7	6	2	8	7
8	2	6	7	8

2. The second best Lo Shu number is called T'IEN YI, which is translated to mean "Doctor from Heaven". This number in the Lo Shu Grid indicates the sector and direction which will bring you upper middle class type of wealth, good friends and three sons ! One may be tempted to regard it as being less favourable than Sheng Chi. In Feng Shui practice, however each of the auspicious and inauspicious Lo Shu numbers have certain explicit uses for which they are best suited, and Tien Yi is exceptionally potent in curing members of the household who may be suffering from prolonged and inexplicable illnesses. If you are suffering from poor health or an illness, this is the direction to activate. Do this by positioning your cooker with its source of energy (the "fire mouth") facing your Tien Yi direction.

 3. The so called third best Lo Shu number is named NIEN YEN which is loosely translated to mean "Longevity with rich descendants". This number identifies the direction and location which best creates harmonious family relationships. If the problem is one of family quarrels, an inability to have children (or sons), or an inability to get married, or if there are constant bickerings between husband and wife, then this is the Lo Shu number which should be activated to correct these family type problems.

 4. The fourth best direction is named FU WEI. This Lo Shu number generally indicates the direction and location which offers a favourable and good life, but with nothing very spectacular in terms of wealth or prosperity. If your main door faces the direction represented by this Lo Shu number or if your bedroom is in the corresponding sector, you will have more boys than girls in your family, and you will make a decent acceptable livelihood. Fu Wei actually corresponds to your KUA number and if you are unable to activate the first three Lo Shu numbers because of landscape or other constraints, then Fu Wei serves to protect you from bad luck and inauspicious Feng Shui.

Each of the "locations" represented by the Lo Shu numbers are referred to as sectors of a house (or office). To identify the sectors, the Lo Shu Grid is superimposed onto layout drawings of the house. These must be carefully delineated. Exact and precise measurements are called for. It is for this reason that Feng Shui Masters strongly advise that houses should have regular (square or rectangular) shapes.

The Lo Shu Grid shown here is sometimes referred to as the Magic Square. It contains the numbers 1 to 9 and these are arranged such that any set of three numbers viewed diagonally, horizotally or vertically adds up to 15, corresponding to the number of days in each of the 24 phases of the solar year.

4	9	2
3	5	7
8	1	6

The Lo-Shu numbers

The Lo Shu pattern of numbers forms the basis of several Chinese cultural symbolisms revolving around the Five Elements and corresponding to the Pa Kua of eight Trigrams organized in the Later Heaven Arrangement.

According to legend, the Lo Shu pattern of numbers was given to mankind on the back of a Great Tortoise which emerged from the River Lo sometime around 2205 BC. It is believed that the profound secrets of the Lo Shu numbers provide much of the foundation of powerful Taoist magic. Indeed many of the ancient mystical rituals of Taoism are synchronised according to the sequence of the nine numbers within the Lo Shu Grid.

Each of these numbers correspond to one of the eight Trigrams in the Later Heaven Arrangement Pa Kua (with the number 5 in the centre). These numbers each fit one of 8 compass directions, and this conveys the profound association of the Lo Shu with the Pa Kua.

This affiliation is reflected in the illustration of the Pa Kua shown in the following page.

The relevant location/sector indicated by the Lo Shu number is determined by superimposing the Lo Shu square onto the layout of a house using the compass directions as a guide. The example sketched below show how this is done, thereby locating the auspicious rooms or sectors of the house in accordance to the relevant Lo Shu number of its owner.

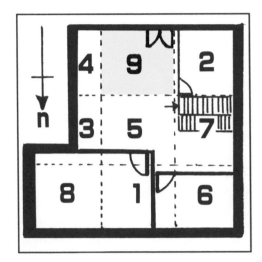

4	9	2
3	5	7
8	1	6

The Lo-Shu Square.

EXAMPLE:

The Lo Shu Grid on the right, with its nine numbers is superimposed onto the layout plan above right, according to compass directions corresponding to the Trigrams in the Later Heaven Pa Kua. Therefore if your best Lo Shu number is 9, your bedroom should be located in the shaded sector, and your main door should face south. Please note that you stand INSIDE the house to determine the compass direction. Likewise your bedroom should be above the shaded sector and your sleeping position should be oriented with your head pointing south. There are many other applications which are dealt with in a later section.

USING THE LATER HEAVEN PA KUA

The next step in the exercise is to establish the lucky or favoured *directions*. This stage in the use of the formula unites the Lo Shu Grid with the Later Heaven Sequence Pa Kua, such that the Grid is now superimposed onto the Pa Kua. Each sector of the Lo Shu corresponds to one of the eight Trigrams of the Pa Kua and these Trigrams are arranged around the Pa Kua according to the Later Heaven Sequence (hence its name).

Each Trigram has its corresponding compass direction and these are the directions that are interpreted as auspicious if the said Lo Shu number has been identified as auspicious. Thus whenever reference is made to a Lo Shu number one is able to immediately identify the corresponding direction. These matching directions do not change because they are determined by the relevant Trigram which occupies each of the Lo Shu sectors. Thus the significance of the Later Heaven and not the Former Sequence of arrangement of the Trigrams.

The Pa Kua shown below has been divided into nine chambers according to the Lo Shu Grid, with the relevant numbers "matching" each of the compass directions. From the way the Trigrams have been arranged, it is possible to do this, ie match each of the numbers of the nine boxes in the Lo Shu Grid with a direction. Please observe that the number 5 which is usually associated with the centre box is not applicable at this stage of the formula.

The Later Heaven Sequence of the Trigrams and their compass directions are matched with Lo Shu Box numbers as follows:

Lo Shu Box 9 = Trigram Li = SOUTH.
Lo Shu Box 7 = Trigram Tui = WEST.
Lo Shu Box 1 = Trigram Kan = NORTH.
Lo Shu Box 3 = Trigram Chen = EAST.

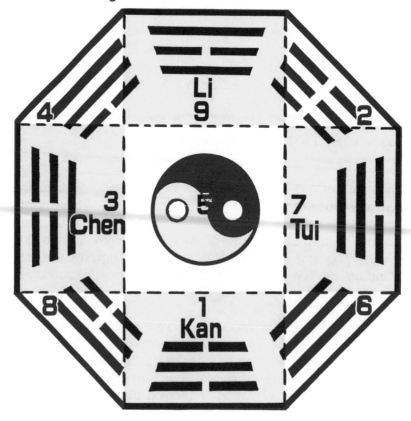

Lo Shu Box 2 = Trigram Kun = SOUTH-WEST.
Lo Shu Box 6 = Trigram Chien = NORTH-WEST.
Lo Shu Box 8 = Trigram Ken = NORTH-EAST.
Lo Shu Box 4 = Trigram Sun = SOUTH-EAST.

As previously indicated eight directions are considered significant. Four of these represent the Primary directions and four represent the secondary directions. In Compass Direction Feng Shui all eight directions carry equal importance. For the individual, four of these directions are good directions while four of them are harmful.

The object is for the practitioner to discover which are his four best and which are his four worst directions. Once one knows one's auspicious and inauspicious directions, one will be able to orientate the compass bearings of homes and dwellings to generate maximum good fortune while at the same time avoiding those directions that create bad fortune.

According to Compass Direction Feng Shui texts, mankind is divided into two groups, people of the East group and people of the the West group. It is believed that those within the same group are more compatible with each other than two people from different groups.

If the husband and wife "belong" to the same group it is also easier to design their homes and bedrooms, since basically the same directions and the same locations within the home will be suitable for both.

It is important to remind readers that the extent of compatibility or incompatibility also depends on other "factors", including the relevant Elements and the Animal symbols of the people concerned.

Compass grouping as a measure of compatibility represent only one indication and is therefore not absolute.

DETERMINING AUSPICIOUS DIRECTIONS ☆

To find your four best directions, refer to Table 3 (again 3A for males and 3B for females). The four "best" directions are given in descending order of their "lucky significance" in these two tables.

TABLE 3A (for MALES)
DETERMINING YOUR BEST COMPASS DIRECTIONS.

YOUR KUA NUMBER	YOUR VERY BEST DIRECTION	YOUR 2ND BEST DIRECTION	YOUR 3RD BEST DIRECTION	YOUR 4TH BEST DIRECTION
1	southeast	east	south	north
3	south	north	southeast	east
4	north	south	east	southeast
9	east	southeast	north	south
5	northeast	west	northwest	southwest
2	northeast	west	northwest	southwest
6	west	northeast	southwest	northwest
7	northwest	southwest	northeast	west
8	southwest	northwest	west	northeast

TABLE 3B (for FEMALES)
DETERMINING YOUR BEST COMPASS DIRECTIONS

YOUR KUA NUMBER	YOUR VERY BEST DIRECTION	YOUR 2ND BEST DIRECTION	YOUR 3RD BEST DIRECTION	YOUR 4TH BEST DIRECTION
1	southeast	east	south	north
3	south	north	southeast	east
4	north	south	east	southeast
9	east	southeast	north	south
5	southwest	northwest	west	northeast
2	northeast	west	northwest	southwest
6	west	northeast	southwest	northwest
7	northwest	southwest	northeast	west
8	southwest	northwest	west	northeast

EXAMPLE ONE: If your KUA number is 6 and you are a female, your best direction is west; your second best direction is northeast, your third best direction is south west and your fourth best direction is northwest. You belong to the West group.

EXAMPLE TWO: if your KUA number is 3, and you are male, your best direction is south, your second best direction is north, your third best direction is southeast, and your fourth best direction is east. You belong to the East group.

Once you have determined your "best" locations and "directions", you will be in a position to considerably improve the Feng Shui of your home, the rooms you occupy, your business premises, your office and your work area ... you can also develop the habit of always sitting in your most favourable direction when negotiating a deal or conducting an interview, when studying or taking an exam; when playing a game of mahjong or making a bet, when submitting an application or when writing a report.

Compass Direction Pa Kua Lo Shu Feng Shui's potency originate from the belief that by aligning your compass directions and that of your abode according to the Lo Shu numbers of your year of birth allows your personal energy flows ie the human Chi in your body to be harmoniously aligned with the Chi of the environment, thereby creating excellent Chi flows which bring abundant good luck.

The more your surroundings are oriented according to your best directions, and the more you do your work and situate your bedroom according to your best locations, the more abundant good luck comes your way.
In applying this concept however you will find it is not always possible to tap your very best directions or your best locations. In such situations, you are advised to use the other three "lucky" directions indicated from the formula. There is thus a certain amount of flexibility.

As has been indicated above, the Feng Shui text describes the best direction as Sheng Chi. If you are fortunate enough to be able to orientate all the rooms that you personally use, as well as the direction of your main door, your sleeping position and so forth in accordance with your luckiest direction, the Text promises that you will have excellent Feng Shui, and your life will be filled with great abundance, prosperity and happpiness. Master Yap often jokes that the man who

YOUR KUA NUMBER	4th Worst Lo Shu No. (HO HAI)	3rd Worst Lo Shu No. (Wu Kuei)	2nd Worst Lo Shu No. (Lui Sha)	Very worst Lo Shu No. ChuehMing
1	7	8	6	2
3	2	6	8	7
4	6	2	7	8
9	8	7	2	6
5	3	4	9	1
2	3	4	9	1
6	4	3	1	9
7	1	9	4	3
8	9	1	3	4

TABLE 4B: WORST LO SHU NUMBERS FOR FEMALES

KUA NUMBER	4th Worst Lo Shu No	3rd Worst Lo Shu No.	2nd Worst Lo Shu No.	Very worst Lo Shu No.
1	7	8	6	2
3	2	6	8	7
4	6	2	7	8
9	8	7	2	6
5	9	1	3	4
2	3	4	9	1
6	4	3	1	9
7	1	9	4	3
8	9	1	3	4

is able to tap his best direction all the time without simultaneously getting hurt by Sha Chi caused by poison arrows, or by inauspicious placements of mountains and waterways will become a multi millionaire in every sense of the word !

The first best direction is therefore considered extremely lucky.

The second best direction (described as "Tien Yi") is excellent if one is ill or suffering from health ailments like back-aches, head-aches, migraines, extreme pain in body organs or even serious illnesses. The way to tap into its potency is to re-align one's bedroom location within the house and also change one's sleeping position such that this second best direction is being "tapped."

The third best direction (Nien Yen) is an excellent direction to use for the entrance door into the family room or bedroom if what is wanted is family harmony since Nien Yen generally promotes goodwill, tolerance and harmonious relationships.

The fourth best direction (Fu Wei) refers to "one's basic self". While it may be ranked fourth in importance for the purpose of generating luck, it is nevertheless a very good direction to use when attempting to improve one's thinking and clear-headedness. This direction enhances personal abilities and capabilities and is therefore particularly suitable for professional executives and managers when they are seated at their desks at work. Similiarly this direction is also recommended for students when they are studying for exams or working on their written work.

DETERMINING BAD LOCATIONS & DIRECTIONS ✱

To find out the four locations and directions that are harmful to one's life, consult Table 4 (Again 4A for males and 4B for females) and Table 5.

As in the case of the auspicious Lo Shu numbers these four "harmful" numbers and compass directions are ranked in ascending order of harmfulness, and like the previous case utilises the Lo Shu Grid and the Later Heaven Sequence Pa-Kua to indicate relevant locations and compass directions.

TABLE 5A: (for MALES)
DETERMINING YOUR WORST COMPASS DIRECTIONS

YOUR KUA NUMBER.	YOUR 4TH WORST DIRECTION	YOUR 3RD WORST DIRECTION	YOUR 2ND WORST DIRECTION	YOUR VERY WORST DIRECTION
1	west	northeast	northwest	southwest
3	southwest	northwest	northeast	west
4	northwest	southwest	west	northeast
9	northeast	west	southwest	northwest
5	east	southeast	south	north
2	east	southeast	south	north
6	southeast	east	north	south
7	north	south	southeast	east
8	south	north	east	southeast

TABLE 5B: (for FEMALES)
DETERMINING YOUR WORST COMPASS DIRECTIONS

YOUR KUA NUMBER	YOUR 4TH WORST DIRECTION	YOUR 3RD WORST DIRECTION	YOUR 2ND WORST DIRECTION	YOUR VERY WORST DIRECTION
1	west	northeast	northwest	southwest
3	southwest	northwest	northeast	west
4	northwest	southwest	west	northeast
9	northeast	west	southwest	northwest
5	south	north	east	southeast
2	east	southeast	south	north
6	southeast	east	north	south
7	north	south	southeast	east
8	south	north	east	southeast

EXAMPLE 1: If you are a female and your KUA Number is 3, then your worst Lo Shu numbers are 2, 6, 8, and 7, with 7 being your worst number ie location in the Lo Shu Grid. From these numbers you can find out that your corresponding bad luck directions are South-West, North-West, North-East and West, with West being your worst direction.

EXAMPLE 2: If you are male and your KUA number is 5, then your most inauspicious Lo Shu numbers are 3, 4, 9, and 1, with 1 being your worst number or location in the Lo Shu Grid. Again from these numbers you will see that your corresponding bad directions are East, South-East, South and North, with North being your worst direction.

These four inauspicious directions are not equally "bad". Like their auspicious counterparts they too have names which describe the consequences of aligning your main door or bedroom etc in these directions. The bad directions are:

1. HO HAI translated as "accidents and mishaps". This is a direction which leads to disaster, but not the kind of disaster which spells the end of everything eg. if you are sleeping with your head aligned in this direction, you might lose a small court case, or you might win although you will lose some money. This is the least bad of the four bad directions.

2. WU KUEI translated as the "five ghosts". This is the second worst of the four bad directions, and if the main door of your house is aligned to face this direction for instance, all your employees will leave you. You could suffer from Fire and Burglary, and in severe cases, your youngest child could get hurt. Aligning your important sectors and directions according to Wu Kuei result in many quarrels within the household and you will not have a peaceful environment at home or at work. On the other hand you can suppress the ill effects of Wu Kuei by locating your toilet or your kitchen in the Wu Kuei sector of the house.

3. LIU SHA or the Six Killings, the third worst position and direction cause grievous harm to the family and to the family business. There will be legal problems in business and family members will constantly get ill, and there could even be death. Feng Shui Masters often recommend locating toilets in the this sector to suppress the bad Chi of the sector.

Chueh
***Ming**

4. CHUEH MING or Total Loss is the Lo Shu number which represents the very worst direction and location. If your main door is facing your Chueh Ming position you will lose all your descendants; your children and grandchildren will die, and your family name will come to an end. You could also lose your wealth, and everything in your life will go wrong. Your family will suffer from regular and persistent problems of ill health. Avoid this direction at all costs. It is both deadly and fatal.

EXAMPLE: Kua number: 8 (Male)
Your best directions are: S.West, N.West, West and N.East.
Your worst directions are: South, North, East and S.East.
Your best Lo Shu Numbers/sectors are: 2, 6, 7, and 8.
Your worst Lo Shu numbers/sectors are: 9,1,3 and 4.

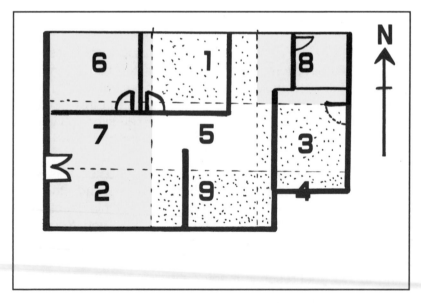

* The best sector in the house for the owner are the shaded areas
❋ He should avoid sleeping or working in the dotted sectors.

The above shows the most basic way of using the Pa-Kua Lo-Shu system of Feng Shui. Having understood this fundamental usage of the system, one can delve deeper into other applications, and also use it in consonance with interpretations of element compatability and landscape (or Form school) Feng Shui.

PART THREE
PRACTICAL APPLICATIONS

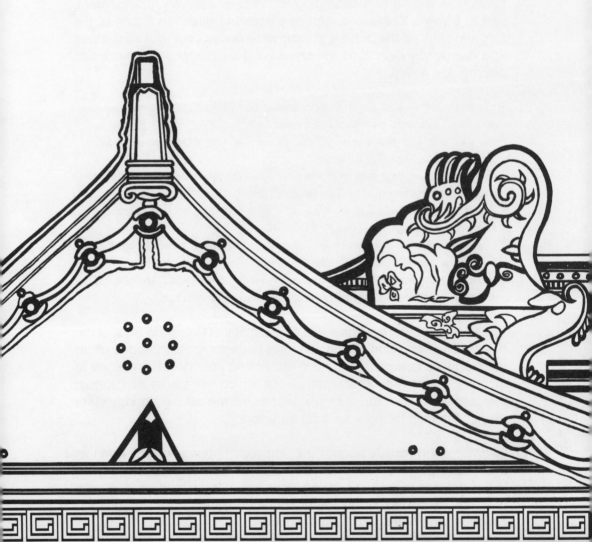

CHAPTER FOUR

FORMULA APPLICATIONS

USING THE PA-KUA DIRECTIONS

There are eight major directions to a house or building. These are taken from the Pa Kua according to the Later Heaven Arrangement, which, being a Chinese compass places the direction South at the top, and North at the bottom. Having determined your four auspicious and four deadly directions, the checklist of orientations which you can activate are as follows:

* *the main door of your house or office should face at least one of your auspicious directions, preferably your Sheng Chi direction.*
* *the door into your bedroom should also face one of your auspicious directions, preferably your Nien Yen direction.*
* *the fire mouth of your oven or cooker should face one of your auspicious directions preferably your Sheng Chi or Tien Yi directions.*
* *you should sit at your desk or office table facing one of your four auspicious directions, preferably your Sheng Chi direction.*
* *when you travel on business or for important matters, you should be travelling from one of your auspicious directions.*
* *when you move house or relocate to another country, you should travel FROM one of your auspicious directions, preferably your Sheng Chi direction.*

The above summarises the major applications of Compass School Pa-Kua Lo Shu Feng Shui. Once you have become accustomed to using the magnetic compass and have committed your good directions to memory, there are other applications which will begin to suggest themselves to you, for example, when you are taking an important examination, sit facing your best direction.

Likewise when you are attending an important interview which involves a scholarship or a job that you want, or you are negotiating an important agreement, or facing your boss, or attending a crucial meeting, try to tap some Feng Shui luck by engineering a sitting direction that faces your best direction.

In using the directions for any of the purposes mentioned, it is recommended that the practitioner purchase a good western type compass. Just remember that western compasses conventionally positions the direction North at the top of the compass, while Chinese compasses place North at the bottom. It is probably more authentic to use a Chinese Luo-Pan geomancer's compass but this is not really necessary.

At this juncture, it might be worthwhile to mention that for purposes of Feng Shui, due account must be taken of shifts in the Earth's magnetic field. Professional Feng Shui men recognise the distinction between the "true north" and the "magnetic north", and they unequivocally maintain that it is the magnetic north which is sensitive to Feng Shui's Chi currents. Some Masters even go to the extent of carefully examining the prevailing magnetic field of a location with special gadgets, taking note of localised variations caused by the geology of the terrain.

Other Masters scoff at such meticulous details. They take a more practical approach and offer a more standard explanation. To begin with, they say, using an ordinary western made compass which uses a magnetic needle to indicate compass directions already takes sufficient account of the earth's magnetic field.

When aligning doors, sitting and sleeping positions, it is then sufficient to vary one's direction by about one to two degrees instead of facing directly or straight at the relevant auspicious direction. This, it is maintained allows the individual to make allowances for the fact that the Chi flowing directly from one's auspicious direction may be too strong. Shifting a couple of degrees to the left or right moderates the effect of the "too strong Chi" while still allowing the auspicious direction to be tapped.

Finally, please note that while in theory, it appears fairly straightforward to understand the formulations that make up the Pa-Kua Lo-Shu system of Feng Shui, the Texts do warn about the initial difficulties involved in putting many of the procedures into practice. In the beginning some of the applications can appear confusing, especially since landscape terrain and Element inter-actions have also to be taken account of. There are also some exceptions to generalised rules in the use of the auspicious directions. However with practice, Feng Shui mystique soon unravels itself.

The text on ....
MAIN DOOR
ORIENTATIONS

If your KUA number is...	.....and your MAIN DOOR is facing:
6	* *Southwest, you'll be rich & prosperous.* * *Northeast or West, you & your descendants will be extremely prosperous and wealthy.*
2	* *Northwest, husband & wife will be harmonious.* * *Northeast or West, get honour from the king.*
8	* *West, you will have a lot of descendants.* * *Northwest & Southwest, your house will be filled with wealth, prosperity and gold.*
7	* *Northeast, your family will be prosperous.* * *Northwest & Southwest, your ancestors' property will grow and expand under your care.*
3	* *Southeast, you will gain promotion quickly and lots of good children.* * *South & North, you get fame and riches quickly.*
4	* *East, your family will have brilliant scholars.* * *South or North, your prosperity will last.*
1	* *South, your cupboard is full of food & money.* * *East & Southeast, lots of descendants.*
9	* *North, plenty of gold and silver for the family.* * *East & Southeast, you will have intelligent sons.*

MAIN DOOR ORIENTATIONS

The conventional interpretation on the use of directions to determine the orientation of the Main Door (ie "where you step in and out" each day) is to try and make it face your best directions. This means pointing the compass from inside the house or building such that the direction you are facing (outwards) should be the direction to use. This is illustrated in the sketch here.

Suppose your best direction is southwest, (ie you belong to the West group, and your KUA number is 8), then your front or main door should be oriented to face southwest, marked A in the diagram.

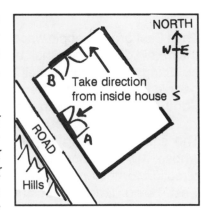

If by facing this southwest direction you find yourself facing a hill, or a straight road or any of the "poison arrows" which bring bad Chi into the house, then select your second best or other good directions. In this case the second best will be northwest or the door marked B in the diagram.

Generally, the accepted practice is to reserve the main Door orientation for the Master or patriarch of the household, unless for some reason he is not the breadwinner or supporter of the family. Tapping the Sheng Chi direction (ie the most auspicious) direction is supposed to help create abundant money luck and bring about other favourable opportunities and events. However, if this is not possible, using the other good luck directions will also bring about good Feng Shui. If there are other members of the household whose KUA number identifies southwest as their worst or inauspicious direction, the Feng Shui master generally recommends the opening of another door, ie a side door which can be used more frequently by the person(s) affected.

There seems, however to be one important exception to the above rule. According to the Feng Shui Text, "if you belong to the West group, you must not live in an East house; and if you belong to the East group you must not live in a West house".

The text defines an East house as a house which faces any of the West Group directions ie North-west, South-west, North-east and West.

It defines a West house as a house which faces any of the East group directions ie South-east, east, South or North.

From the stipulation above, it then appears that there will be some people in the East and West groups who will be unable to "tap" their Sheng Chi directions for the siting of their main Door since for them, by doing so would mean countering this rule.

Thus East group people whose KUA numbers are 1 or 9, cannot allow their main door to face their best direction ie South-east or East since by doing so will render their homes "West" homes. Only East group people whose KUA numbers are 3 or 4 may use their best directions South and North as both are East group directions.

The same reasoning applies for West group people. Only those whose KUA numbers are 2, 5, and 8 are able to use their best direction for their main door. This is because North-east and South-west, being directly opposite each other allow them to face a West group direction, and still be deemed to be staying in a West group house. This rule is initially a little confusing. The sketches below should help in understanding it.

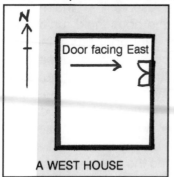

A WEST HOUSE

The diagram on the left shows a West group house because the front door is facing East. This, according to the Text, automatically places the house in the West sector. This house is thus "more suitable" for people who belong to the West group.

The diagram on the right illustrates an East group house because

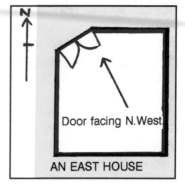

Door facing N.West

AN EAST HOUSE

the front door is facing North-west. This "places" the house in the East sector because North-west is directly opposite South-east which is an east group direction. The defination of an east or west house is therefore directly related to the orientation of the front door.

OTHER DOOR ORIENTATIONS

The orientation of all other doors within the house should theoretically also face the owner's best direction. This, obviously is seldom practical. Feng Shui Texts dealing with the Compass School's Pa Kua Lo Shu System suggest that each of the bedroom doors for example would be better oriented to serve the actual occupant of the bedroom.

Thus sons and daughters have different auspicious directions from their parents, and it would therefore be useful to investigate their respective Lo Shu numbers to determine their good directions.

A second consideration is the actual direction itself. The Text suggests that because bedrooms deal with family harmony and relationships, rather than using the Sheng Chi direction it is sometimes advisable to use the Nien Yen (or third best) direction. This encourages the family Chi to "rise" thereby creating peace and harmony in the household, especially between spouses. Orienting the bedroom door in the Nien Yen direction also assists childless couples to have children, and those who yearn for sons to have their wish granted.

Yet another application suggested addresses households whose occupants constantly get sick, or where illnesses are persistent. In such cases activating the Tien Yi (or second best) direction for the person thus afflicted does help in alleviating the condition. Tien Yi means "doctor from heaven" and utilising this direction when used in conjunction with other measures like adjusting the oven fire-mouth (dealt with later) apparently helps.

Certain portions of the Text also imply that sometimes the Element of the Main Door can be "strengthened", with the addition of another door with either a similiar Element or with an Element that helps create it. For example if one's main door is facing the direction South which has Fire as its Element, then locating another side door facing South-east which symbolises small Wood will be auspicious, since Wood produces Fire, allowing it to burn with added brilliance. In addition, both South and South-east are East group directions thereby there is no clash of directions for the occupant. The important guideline here is always go back and check your four good directions before beginning to refine the details with analyses of the Elements.

DESK and WORK ORIENTATIONS

One of the more important ways of activating good Feng Shui is to inspect the direction which you are facing each time you sit down at your desk to study, or to work when in the office. It is believed that if the sitting position allows you to be facing your most auspicious directions, your mind will be clear and your decisions will mostly be good decisions. Sitting in your Sheng Chi or Fu Wei directions also assist you in making the kind of judgements which will enable you to prosper and advance in your work or career.

In applying this principle do take note that it is the direction you are facing which is to be activated. This is shown in the diagram below.

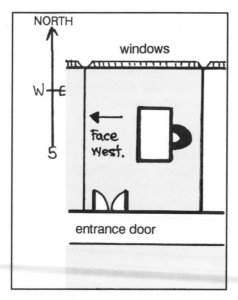

The office shown here is occupied by a lady lawyer whose KUA number is 5. Her auspicious directions are SW, NW, W and NE. She is sitting at her desk facing West which is her Nien Yen direction. She cannot sit facing SouthWest because this would force her to have her back to the window, a situation which is not recommended since this means a lack of support.

She can also sit facing the other two of her good directions ie NW and NE but as shown from the layout, this forces her to position her desk at an angle, which is acceptable; but her Nien Yen direction fits the decor and orientation of her office very well.

Good desk orientation also contributes to the harmony of your working life. If you are a manager, facing your Nien Yen position will result in you having few problems with your staff, and certainly you will not have major problems involving dreaded office politics.

The author has applied this method of practising Feng Shui on countless occasions, since she has been in possession of her auspicious directions for many years. The first time she used it was when she was assigned to negotiate the Malaysian Franchise for Yamaha Motorcycles on behalf of her then employer, the Hong Leong Group. It had been a spur of the moment decision, brought about by the initial resistance of her Japanese counterpart, who, reacting to the fact that she was a woman politely declined to discuss business.

It was potentially a disastrous situation and since she had no intention of flying back to Kuala Lumpur empty handed, she decided to "test" out her direction by slowly shifting her position such that she faced her Sheng Chi direction. (It must be added here that discreetly checking Singapore Shangri La coffee house compass orientations where the first meeting was held took some doing !)

The discussions dragged along painfully but by the next day, still facing her excellent direction, she succeeded in achieving a breakthrough. After several months of negotiations, Yamaha happily appointed the Group as their sole agents for Malaysia and Singapore.

Using one's auspicious directions to gain some mysterious good luck advantage in business negotiations may sound ludicrous, but the reasoning applied by the author in those early days was "what is there to lose, and what does it cost ? ".

Feng Shui is after all a metaphysical science that defies conventional logic. Belief in its potency is a purely personal decision which harms no one, and if it can do some good why not try it ?

Once one overcomes the initial mind block, and acknowledges that directions can bring Feng Shui luck, it is possible to be extremely creative in its many uses. Thus, sit facing your best direction when interviewing for a job, meeting your boss, attending difficult management meetings, preparing an important project proposal, or when trying to think up novel solutions to difficult predicaments or dilemmas. The list of applications can be endless.

For students, sitting in your good directions enable you to study more effectively. Your learning will yeild better and faster results as you succeed not only in "inputing" the facts but can also now effectively "output" all that you have studied during examinations.
Sitting in a good direction at school is also conducive to having a harmonious and balanced school life. Relations with friends, peers and teachers alike will be smooth and harmonious.

OVEN and COOKER FIRE-MOUTH ORIENTATIONS

It is the consensus of the Text and also several Feng Shui Masters, that the positioning of the family cooker or oven has a crucial, and often exceedingly huge impact on the well-being and luck of a family. According to them, even if you succeed in getting everything else right, if your cooker is placed with its fire mouth facing any one of your four deadly directions, then the result will be negative Feng Shui.

The fire mouth describes the source of the power, and when applied to modern family rice cookers, the fire mouth is where the current of electricity comes from. Thus to get your rice cooker facing the correct direction point its incoming plug in your best directions. Pointing it in your Sheng Chi direction brings wealth and prosperity, while pointing it in your Tien Yi direction will improve your health. When it faces your Nien Yen direction, you will have a very pleasant and harmonious family life where there will be little quarrelling and misuderstandings.

Sketch of a conventional stove showing its fire mouth.

fire-
mouth

On the other hand if the fire mouth faces your Chueh Ming direction, it will bring terrible bad luck, sometimes leading to a death or deaths in the family. If oriented to Liu Sha, the "six killings" or Wu Kuei, the "five ghosts", you will get into financial difficulties and even have to cope with legal problems. Facing Ho Huai also portends bad luck.

The negative effect of having the fire mouth face any one of your deadly directions supposedly creates more harm than anything else being wrong (eg like having your main door in the wrong direction). When a household experiences a series of bad luck the cause can usually be traced to the fire mouth facing the wrong direction.

Sketch of modern rice cooker showing its fire mouth

fire-mouth

Business Travel

The Pa-Kua Lo-Shu system of Feng Shui can be used to assign good Feng Shui luck to any important move which involves travelling somewhere, be it an important business trip overseas, a move to a new house, a relocation to a new country, a transfer to a new office or a change of job. Application calls for the practitioner to organise his itinerary such that his direction of travel benefits him.

For this particular application, it is interesting to note that it is NOT the direction one is travelling to that must be attended to. Instead, it is the direction one is coming from that is the crucial direction to take note of. The explanation for this is , "wherever you go, bring good luck with you from your old place".

For example, if you are travelling towards South-west then you will be coming from North-East. In this instance North-east should be your auspicious direction.

And if you are moving South, then you will be coming from the North. In this example, you should make certain that North is one of your good directions.

Obviously it is not possible to change the direction of a destination. For instance if your business trip requires you to travel to Hong Kong from Kuala Lumpur, obviously the "going" direction is North-east, and you will be travelling from South-west. This is something you cannot change. What then if South-west happens to be your Chueh Ming (or worst direction).

The section of the Classical Text dealing with travel directions advise making a detour! Make a detour such that you will arrive in Hong Kong from an auspicious direction.

Thus you could make a stop at cities like Kota Kinabalu (and travel from South to HK); or Taipeh (and travel from North-eastto HK) or even Manila (and travel from South-east to HK). If you examine a map of East and South-east Asia, you will immediately see other possibile routes. When the author was transferred to Hong Kong very suddenly in 1982, she accepted the transfer with a great deal of confidence. It was many years later however before she found out that moving to Hong Kong had allowed her to travel there from one of her good directions. Which was probably the reason why Hong Kong was relatively lucky for her. When she moved to live and work briefly in England however, the situation was not auspicious, and upon checking the direction of travel, it was discovered that travelling direct to England involved a voyage from her worst direction.

Generally, depending on your KUA number and your country of origin, there will be certain continents of the world which are more auspicious for you than others, ie these will be the places where you will be able to travel directly to, from your best direction. It is for this reason that Feng Shui Masters in Hong Kong are often called upon to advise parents whether they should send their children to Australia, Canada, the United States or the United Kingdom for further education.
For the same reason, certain export markets tend to be more lucky than others for a manufacturer businessman.

Relocation Travel
This same principle of travel can also be applied when you are moving to a new house or a new country. Carefully check the direction of travel and make a detour if necessary. Usually the more permanent a move is, the more care must be exercised when "planning"

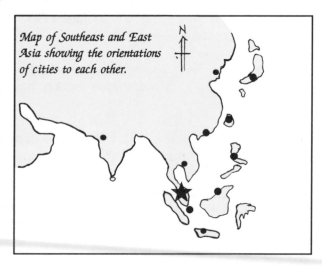

Map of Southeast and East Asia showing the orientations of cities to each other.

out your route. It also makes sense for the husband and wife to travel separately if their KUA numbers differ so that they each can tap into their respective good directions.

Similiarly if you are transferred and the transfer involves a change of office, make sure that on the day you physically move into your new office, your route, either from your house or from your old office augurs well for you from a Feng Shui perspective. Paying insufficient attention to this important detail could have horrendous consequences.

USING THE LO-SHU LOCATIONS

While the directions indicated from Lo-Shu numbers are based on corresponding Trigrams (arranged in the Later Heaven Sequence), the locations symbolised by Lo-Shu numerals are matched by easily super-imposing the Lo-Shu Grid on to layout plans of houses or buildings. The way to do this is to match the compass directions signified by the numerals, and then to fit these directions to the house or building that is being investigated.

The house is then theoretically "divided" into nine sectors to match the Lo-Shu Grid.

This is illustrated in the sketch of a typical layout plan of the ground floor of a medium size house shown here. Notice that the Pa-Kua/Lo-Shu can be "adjusted" to fit the dimensions of the house.

Feng Shui Masters generally recommend that a house or building should, as far

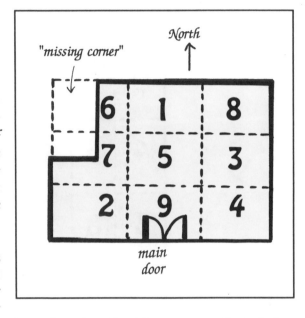

as possible, be regular shaped, and preferably square so that all nine chambers of the Lo-Shu Grid can be represented in the house. Where there are "missing corners" it will be better if these represent your inauspicious sectors. Otherwise adjustments or Feng Shui "cures' like mirrors should be used to symbolically create the corner.

If there is more than one level to the house, each succeeding floor is similiarly "divided" into nine sectors in the same way. When you have done this, you will be ready to identify the rooms and corners in the house which represent your auspicious locations and those which represent your inauspicious locations.

This is why it is always more convenient to incorporate Feng Shui considerations when a house or building is at its planning or drawing stage. One is then able to identify the sectors of the house which are deemed lucky for the residents, and allot these sectors accordingly, ie reserving the auspicious rooms for important rooms like bedrooms, offices, studies and libraries, while ensuring toilets, store rooms and kitchens are sited in the inauspicious sectors.

The sketch on the previous page depicts a house which faces a primary direction (ie its front door is facing South). If a house faces a secondary direction note that the Lo-Shu Grid numerals appear to be "adjusted", as demonstrated in the diagram below.

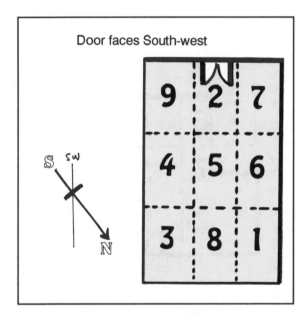

Door faces South-west

If you have to make a similiar "adjustment", always check to make sure that all the numerals are correctly placed. This can be done by matching the numerals against their respective compass directions OR by mentally adding all the numerals in lines of three, vertically, horizontally or diagonally and making sure they add up to 15. If they don't add up to 15, you know a mistake has been made. Incidentally, do remember that the number 5 is always in the centre. This system of Compass School Feng Shui stays nuetral in its comments about this central sector of the Grid. Which could be why most ancient Chinese houses usually have a courtyard located in the centre of their family homes. This is roughly equivalent to the air-wells or internal gardens of modern homes.

From the foregoing, it becomes obvious that when both husband and wife belong to the same East or West group and therefore the same rooms are "good" or "bad" for both of them, it is much easier to organise the rooms to fit both spouses. Should they belong to different groups, some adjustments may be required. Sometimes the differences can be so great, husband and wife may have to occupy different bedrooms in the interests of harmony.

BEDROOM LOCATIONS

Each of the bedrooms in the house should ideally be located in those sectors which best suit the auspicious Lo-Shu numbers of the occupant. If this can be accomodated such that every member of the family succeeds in obtaining his/her best location ie their Sheng Chi location then all members will benefit from excellent Feng Shui.

When this is further intensified by each aligning his/her actual sleeping position in a way which allows his/her head to point in the Sheng Chi direction, and the door into the bedroom also faces Sheng Chi, then very powerful good Feng Shui will be the result. This perfect bedroom orientation and alignment is indicated in the sketch below.

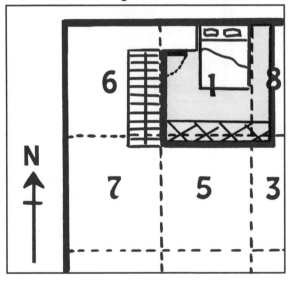

The sketch illustrates the bedroom of a person whose KUA number is 4. From the tables you will see that his Sheng Chi direction is North, and his Sheng Chi Lo-Shu sector is 1. His bedroom, bedroom door and sleeping position are all aligned perfectly. He will benefit from excellent Feng Shui.

It should be evident from the illustration that getting the sector, the sleeping position and the bedroom door all aligned to the North sector and direction is very difficult. Satisfying two out of three may be possible. Satisfying all three requirements is often impossible.

In short, it is seldom practical for everyone in a household to get everything perfect from a Feng Shui perspective. Often, compromises must be made, and some will have to make do with less auspicious directions for some of the requirements. So long as the important orientations are aligned to one of the four lucky directions or locations, Feng Shui is generally regarded as well taken care of.

This is how most Feng Shui Masters decide when advising clients on the locations of rooms, and when they comment on layout plans. In almost all instances efforts are usually made to ensure that the Head of the household benefits from all his good directions.

This sketch here shows part of an upstairs layout with three bedrooms, one of which is in East group sector (marked #) and two are in West group sector (marked *). The bedroom doors and beds face various directions. As an excercise see if you can allocate the rooms to members of your family after checking their KUA numbers, and study whether the door and sleeping directions match the bedrooms, or can be improved upon. The dotted lines show Lo-Shu sector demarcations.

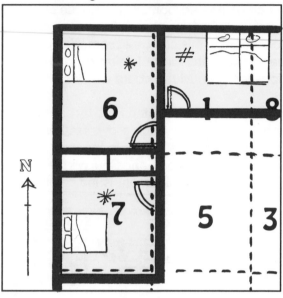

If the auspicious sector corresponding to the Sheng Chi numeral of the Head of the Household is partly missing (due for example to the shape of the house), the solution is to select the second or third best sector ie his Tien Yi or Nien Yen sector. This is better than having his bedroom "spill over" into an inauspicious direction. In this context it is pertinent to explain that while these sectors are described as second or third best, they nevertheless possess other attributes and do activate Chi to benefit households in ways other than bringing monetary prosperity. Tien Yi is good for health while Nien Yen is excellent for marriage and family life.

Finally, it is also necessary to ensure that fairly precise measurements are made at all times to ensure that the integrity of the magic square is maintained. This means that each of the sectors should have approximately the same dimensions or size, and where the house is rectangular or has some parts shorter or narrower than other parts, allowances must be made for these "missing sectors". This often implies drawing imaginary sectors which lie outside the house into the layout plans, as shown in the illustrations.

LOCATION OF TOILETS & KITCHENS

Feng Shui does not assign positive connotations to the household toilets or kitchen. These are designated as areas within the house where washing and cleaning takes place, especially in the toilets where the garbage of the household is flushed away. In view of this, Feng Shui Texts instruct that these rooms must be located in areas of the home which represent any one of the four inauspicious or unlucky sectors. The toilets and kitchen are believed to be able to "press" down on the bad luck and also control any Sha Chi which may be lying in those areas.

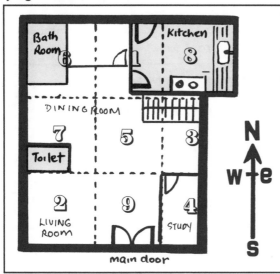

The diagram shows the location of the toilets, bathrooms and kitchen of a person whose KUA number is 3. His inauspicious Lo-Shu numerals, as indicated in the tables are thus 2, 6, 8 and 7. His Chueh Ming sector is 7, so there is a toilet located here in the West. His kitchen is located in 8 (North-east) and his bathroom is located in 6, the North-west.

Toilets are preferably located in the Chueh Ming sector, or failing this in the other unlucky sectors. There could be problems adhering to this requirement if members of the household have different unlucky sectors. In such instances, the Master of the House must be served by using his inauspicious Lo-Shu numbers. It would be unfortunate if the toilets are located in his Sheng Chi position since this implies his good luck is being flushed away.

Kitchens are also to be located in unlucky sectors. Remember that although the kitched must be in an inauspicious location, the fire-mouth of the cooker or oven must be made to face an auspicious direction. Thus even as bad luck is being "burned away" in the unlucky site, the fire-mouth is efficiently attracting abundant good luck.

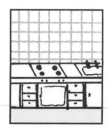

The Text on ....

KITCHEN & OVEN
ORIENTATIONS

If the Kitchen or Oven is in	..........this will be the result:
SHENG CHI	Miscarriage, unpopularity, & no livelihood.
TIEN YI	Will get sick/weak, & difficult to get well.
NIEN YEN	Hard to get married, lots of quarrels.
FU WEI	No money, no longevity, forever poor.
CHUEH MING	Lots of sons, money, servants, good health.
LUI SHA	Family very steady, no disaster, no fire.
HO HAI	Will not lose money, no illness.
wU KUEI	No fire, no robbery, no sickness. Successful.

* The kitchen situation is no small matter. It is the most important thing in the household. If it is located in the good locations it will press on the family's good luck. If it is located in the bad locations it will press on the family's bad luck.

 ON LOCATION OF PONDS..... from the TEXT:
* If you have a pond both at the front and back of the house, young children in the household will find it difficult to survive in that house.
* If the pond is on the left hand side of the door (inside looking out), every generation will prosper and have property.
* If the pond is on the right hand side of the door, the husband is fickle about women and will most likely have several wives

✽ If there is a rock garden directly facing your front or back door, during your bad years you will lose all your money because the rocks are "pressing" you.

One of the luxuries of modern living is that most families have a small study or workroom in their homes, which is used as a mini library or work area. The siting of the study takes on some prominence in Feng Shui considerations because this is where serious work and study take place. Locating this room in a favourable aspect will attract good luck Chi. The best Lo-Shu numeral to use in this case is the Sheng Chi number but the other lucky sectors are also suitable. Inside the study however, arrange the furniture such that you are facing your best direction. Feng Shui Masters also recommend that if you construct bookshelves along the walls, it is best if these are not exposed since the shelves can be interpreted as representing sharp edges which will result in the creation of Sha Chi. Hence use sliding doors to close up the bookcase.

If the study in your house is where your children do most of their studying and homework, then remember to use the Sheng Chi Lo-Shu numeral of your children. This ensures that the room is aspected to suit them, thus creating good Feng Shui for them.

Example:

The sketch on the left shows a study which has been oriented to suit Mr Li's two sons, both of whom belong to the East group. David's KUA number is 4, while Robert's KUA number is 9. Their best directions and Lo-Shu numbers differ but the Study, sited in the Eastern sector of the house (Lo-Shu number 3) is good for both of them. There are two desks inside the study, one facing east (3) for Robert and one facing North (1) for David.

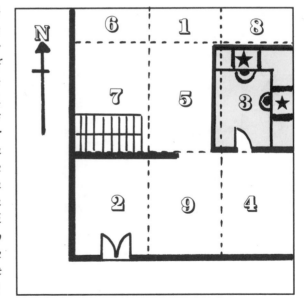

LOCATION OF THE OFFICE and DESK

At work, the exact location of your office or desk is extremely important in determining whether you are able to attract good luck Chi to benefit your career or business. This, together with your sitting direction constitute the two main things to take care of. If possible try to locate your room/desk in the sector of the office which represents your best (Sheng Chi) sector. If this is not possible then try getting your other good luck locations. But do not sit in the corner or part of the office which represents your inauspicious location. When you have ensured that your location is favourable, try to orientate your sitting position such that you are facing your best directions.

While arranging your office situation to tap into your good Lo-Shu sectors and directions do not forget to give due recognition to the presence of poison arrows from angles and sharp corners, and do try to sit in a way which does not require you to have your back to the door or to the window. Remember that the office is not your home. Here you are interfacing with colleagues, employees and bosses. They are not your family, hence the effect of Sha Chi takes on more menacing outlooks. At home you may sit at your desk with your back to the door, but at the office, such an orientation suggests someone "stabbing you in the back." And having your back to the window suggests a lack of support. So do be careful.

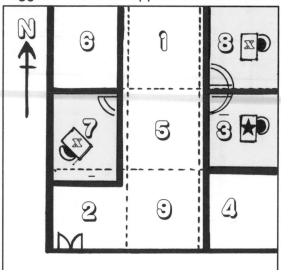

This is the layout of a Sales office.

Rajan, one of the sales executives (KUA number 6) has his room located in sector 3 (East sector), which is inauspicious for him, although he is facing West, his best direction.

If he can change to the rooms marked X in sectors 7 (West) & face northeast, OR 8 (S.West) & still face west, his sales career will improve vastly.

CHAPTER FIVE

CASE STUDIES on the USE OF THE FORMULA

Much of Compass School Feng Shui is based on pre-calculated tables and formula. The doctrines that lie behind these tables must often times be taken at face value. Consequently, as with almost all metaphysical sciences, a fair bit of intellectually stimulated intuition is required. Interpretation of formulas can be difficult. Correlating the theory of a wisdom or an ideology to the practical reality of everyday living is not easy. In the practice of Feng Shui, sometimes the multiplicity of "things to check" can be so overwhelming as to deem the entire exercise tiresome. A great deal of patience is thus required.

The theory of Feng Shui is easy to comprehend. Even the cultural complexities associated with the premier symbols is not beyond most of us, ie the Pa Kua and the Lo Shu; and then again the Yin Yang Cycle and the Wisdom of the I Ching philosophies, not to mention the confusing contradictions of the interactions of the five elements.

Doctrines and the idealogies however are one thing. Practice and efficacy are something else.

In the final analysis it is whether Feng Shui really works that matter; and if it does, how can the average person proceed with the practical applications of Feng Shui.

The author is mindful of these difficulties, having experienced the dilemma of not knowing "exactly" what to do, often enough. How does one impart knowledge of the Feng Shui sciences ?
The author has decided to apply the well known case method approach she learnt at the Harvard Business School years ago, to convey some of the nuances of Feng Shui application using the Lo Shu numbers and Compass directions already determined for each individual. The cases presented are a mixture from old Feng Shui classics, and from Master Yap's memory bank.

CASE 1. THE COURT OFFICIAL
Changing the "fire-mouth" to change one's luck.

There was a Court official, a Mr Tao, who had had a brilliant career in the emperor's court. He had amassed a large fortune, had several concubines and many sons. In his sixtieth year he ordered a new house to be built on the outskirts of the capital, where he planned to live out his retirement and enjoy his many grandchildren. Mr Tao had been a scholar. His personal knowledge of Feng Shui was deep and profound. In planning the house he had also consulted several Feng Shui Masters of different schools and the site of his new home demonstrated all the pre-requisites for a peaceful retirement.

Mr Tao's KUA number was 8. He belonged to the West Group. His Lo Shu numbers were 2,6,7 and 8; and his best compass directions were S.West, N.West, West and N.East. Accordingly the main door to his new home was oriented to face southwest, his best direction. His bedroom was located in the southwest sector of the house and his sleeping position had his head also pointing southwest. The hills around his new home demonstrated the ideal white tiger, green dragon configuration, and in front of his main door a slow meandering river flowed past. From a Feng Shui viewpoint everything was perfect. Six months after he moved in, quarrels erupted in his previously peaceful household. More serious however were the arrest of two of his sons, and he himself became embroiled in a scandal. He was accused of stealing from the Imperial Treasury. He was in serious trouble. The Feng Shui man was sent for. He found everything perfect. Only one thing was wrong. The Fire mouth of the Oven was facing southeast, Mr Tao's Chueh Ming (worst) direction, the one which would cause the death of his family name and his descendants. The location of the kitchen was in Sector 7, Mr Tao's Yuen Nien (good) direction; it was "pressing" on Mr Tao's luck causing family discord.

The Feng Shui Master immediately had the kitchen moved to Sector 4 of the house, Mr Tao's worst sector. This would allow the kitchen to "press" away all the bad luck. He also changed the oven mouth to face southwest. Within 3 months Mr Tao was cleared of all charges, his sons were released and harmony returned to his family.

 LESSON TO BE LEARNT:
* Always check the fire mouth direction of the family oven.
* Do not locate the kitchen in your good sectors.

CASE 2. THE VILLAGE SCHOOL
Balancing the Elements of the Pa Kua.

This is the case of a village school in Southern China. For years the school was renowned for producing excellent scholars who went on to pursue successful careers and brought prosperity to the village. One year, the school authorities decided to expand their facilities and built a new library. The new structure was situated behind the main building, on the west side. Soon thereafter, the school experienced disastrous results for its students. This unfortunate trend continued for three years, reaching a crisis when student enrollment dropped drastically. The Feng Shui man was called in. It was soon obvious to the old Master that the excellent Feng Shui of the School had been destroyed with the construction of the new library. "Drastic measures are called for", he told the Authorities. "Do what needs to be done", the Village Head replied. The Feng Shui Master did three things, and thereafter the School prospered once more. Its students regained their past glory and went on to achieve even greater successes.

WHAT THE FENG SHUI MAN DID:
The new library was located in the WEST, whose KUA element is METAL. The building was taller than the main school whose main door was located on the East. Thus the Metal of the West was killing the Wood of the East.

1. The Master opened a new door in the South East (also Wood) to supplement the wood of the main door, thereby strengthening the Chi of the front door. (Marked as A in the diagram). 2. He also built a Pagoda higher than the library in the North. The element of North is water. This absorbs the energy of the Metal and supplies water for the Wood, thus activating the doors. (Marked as B in the diagram) 3. He then built a gazebo in the South of the main building to represent Fire which controls the metal. The Wood also supplies the Fire to produce light, thus creating "brilliance" for the school's Chi. (marked C in the diagram).

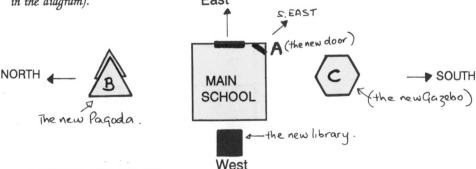

LESSON TO BE LEARNT:
* Never forget to consider the Elements of the Pa Kua & their relationships.

CASE 3: THE MAN WHO YEARNED FOR SONS
Using the Lo Shu numbers to enhance family life

There was a very wealthy man who at the age of fifty still had no sons. His wife had been unsuccessful at conceiving and was completely against the idea of his taking any concubines. In desperation he agreed to let the Feng Shui master investigate his house. The man's KUA number was 5, and his Lo Shu numbers were 8, 7, 6, and 2.

The Feng Shui Master discovered that both his kitchen and his toilet were located in the Yuen Nien sector of his house ie Sector 6, corresponding to the North West part of his house. The Feng Shui man explained that the toilet and the oven were "pressing" down his "family sector". This Nien Yen sector, the Feng Shui master explained, was the most crucial Lo Shu number for bringing harmony into family life. Having his Nien Yen sector crushed had created detrimental consequences for the man. He had no descendants to carry on his family name, a situation which causes much anxiety to the Chinese. So the Master shifted the toilet and the kitchen out of the No 6 sector, and re-located them into the No.1 sector, ie in the northern corner of the house. This would ensure that it was the Chueh Ming Sector (his worst sector) which would get crushed.

Within a year the man had found himself seven concubines who each produced him a son. His wife did not object. The Feng Shui Master had advised him to take as concubines only those women whose KUA number coincided with his best Lo Shu Number ie the number 8. All his concubines thus belonged to the West group (like him) and all of them were deemed good Feng Shui for him.

The sketch shows the relocation of the kitchen and the toilet from the No 6 sector to the no 1 sector of the house. The corresponding directions are also indicated for ease of reference.

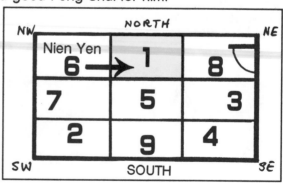

LESSON TO BE LEARNT:
For all family related matters check on or activate your Nien Yen Lo Shu sector.

CASE 4: LOOKING FOR A WIFE
Activating the Nien Yen sector

Ta Khor was the eldest son in a family of three boys. Because his father was an old fashioned man, he would not allow his two younger sons to marry until after the eldest son, Ta Khor had found a wife. Unfortunately, while his two brothers had serious girlfriends and were ready for marriage Ta Khor had great difficulty even in finding himself a lady friend, let alone get married. The situation came to a head when the second son threatened to defy his father's wishes.

To resolve the problem and avert a family crisis, Ta Khor's mother decided to consult a Feng Shui Master to find a solution to the dilemma. Ta Khor's KUA number was 6. This meant that his auspicious Lo Shu numbers were 7, 8, 2 and 6, and his best directions were West, N.East, S.West and N.West. The Feng Shui Master advised the family to move the oven such that its "fire mouth" ie the mouth of the oven, was facing Ta Khor's Nien Yen direction, which in his case was No. 2 or the compass direction South-West. In addition he advised Ta Khor to move his room to a room which was located southwest of his parents' room. The Feng Shui Master promised he would be married within a few months, and at any rate would not have to wait longer than three years.

The necessary changes were made. Ta Khor did indeed succeed in finding himself a wife within a few months. On the advice of the Feng Shui Master his wife's KUA number corresponded to his first Lo Shu number, ie the number 7. The match was thus deemed "suitable".

The sketch shows the movement southwest of his parents' room. If it is not possible to "move" towards your Nien Yen direction, which in this case is south-west, then the parents are advised to change their rooms to make the move possible. ie if getting the son or daughter married is the objective !

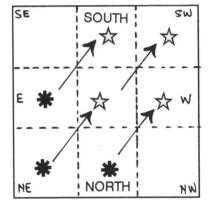

LESSON TO BE LEARNT:
Use different Lo Shu Sectors to achieve different objectives.
Check earlier sections of this chapter.

CASE 5: THE HAPPY MERCHANT
Beware of the "Five Ghosts"

Mr Loh was a popular merchant who lived just outside Canton. He had a successful business buying and selling a variety of household and wooden products. His KUA number was 4, and he had married a woman whose KUA number was 1 (which corresponded to his very best Lo Shu number). It was a perfect match and they were very happy. The Union was blessed with 5 sons.

Some years later, he decided to enlarge his house, and this was when his problems started. Inadvertently and by mistake, Mr Loh shifted the position of his oven, and in so doing turned his oven's fire mouth to face southwest (or Lo Shu number 2). This was his Wu Kuei or Five Ghosts direction. Worst still it was also his wife's Chueh Ming (worst) direction. As if that was not bad enough Mr Loh also changed the direction of his main door, also to the Wu Kuei direction.

The outcome was a major tragedy. Mr and Mrs Loh lost all five sons. It was quite by chance that Mr Loh met up with master Qi, a local Feng Shui Master who was well schooled in the Pa Kua Lo Shu method. Upon arriving at the house, he immediately diagnosed the problem, and proceeded to make several changes.

First the Master re-located the kitchen to the southwest sector of the house (Sector 2), the Wu Kuei sector to "press" on the 5 ghosts.

Next he turned the oven such that its fire mouth faced the Nien Yen direction, ie North.

Then he changed the main door so that it faced the Tien Yi direction ie South.

Within a few months, Mr Loh's wife became pregnant and delivered a son the following year. Eventually Mr and Mrs Loh got three more sons.

LESSONS TO BE LEARNT:
* Try to refrain from making major changes to your house if things are going well for you and your family.
* If you do decide to make renovations to your house, check both the good directions as well as the bad directions to ensure you do not inadvertently activate the "Five Ghosts" or the "Six Killings"

CASE 6: THE SON WHO STAYED AWAY TOO LONG
Using Feng Shui to re-unite the family

Mrs Chan, a widow had spent her entire life working as a washerwoman to send her only son through school and University. Cheng Ho was a very bright boy. Studying by candle light he lived up to his mother's expectations and made good. After graduating as an Engineer, Cheng Ho bought a small link house in one of the new housing estates in Petaling Jaya. Mother and son moved to the new house. Mrs Chan was estatic. Shortly thereafter, Cheng Ho won a scholarship to undertake further studies in the United States.

He soon graduated with high honours. Mrs Chan was overjoyed, and excitedly prepared for his return. But Cheng Ho had other plans. Instead of coming back, he took a job in California, married an American born Chinese, had two children and settled down there. The years passed. Although he faithfully sent money to his mother, Cheng Ho made it clear he had no desire to come home nor did it occur to him to bring his mother to see her grandchildren in the United States. Letters from him were few and far between. Living by herself, Mrs Chan ached with unhappiness, but was too proud to let her son know her true feelings. She knew in her heart that he might never return, that she might even die without seeing her grandchildren. The thought of the lonely years stretching ahead filled her with dread. It was around this time that she met Master Yap. When she confided her apprehensions to him, Master Yap offered to see what he could do. He discovered her KUA number was 3.

Upon reaching her house, he proceeded to change the position of her oven such that the fire mouth faced South East, her Nien Yen direction. He also changed her main door to face this same direction and advised her to move to another bedroom which corresponded to Lo Shu number 4, also her Nien Yen location.

Seven months later Mrs Chan rang Master Yap to let him know that Cheng Ho had written her to say he was "bringing his family on a visit home". After that first trip back, Cheng Ho eventually returned to Malaysia for good. Coincidence or Feng Shui ?

LESSON TO BE LEARNT:
Do not under-estimate the potency of Feng Shui.

CASE 7: THE SICK AND FEEBLE YOUNGSTERS
Checking a child's Lo Shu numbers & elements for healthy living

* There was the case of a father whose KUA number was 7. He had a son whose Kua number was 3. This coincided with the father's worst Lo Shu number or Chueh Ming. This number represented the death of "all descendants" and it was obvious to the Feng Shui Master who came to the house that the father's Lo Shu number was literally "killing" his son. So the Master checked the son's favourable Lo Shu numbers and found out that the son's Nien Yen number was 4, which correspond to south-east. He succeeded in persuading the father to let the son stay in a different house, (with his uncle) which lay in the direction equivalent to south-east of his father's house. This also had the effect of the father being north-west of the son, ie No 6, which coincided with the father's best direction ie Sheng Chi. The son recovered and grew into a healthy young man and the father's fortune also prospered from the Sheng Chi being "sent" to him by the son.

* Another story tells of a new born baby perpetually crying into the night. The child was also purging and constantly had indigestion. The mother tried every kind of medicine to treat the child, to no avail. Eventually, she consulted a Feng Shui Master. The child belonged to the West Group and his KUA number was 2. Both the sectors 2 (SW) and 8 (NE) which represented his good sectors symbolised Earth. Both his parents belonged to the East Group. Their KUA number was 4 which symbolised Wood. The main door of the house and the oven mouth had been oriented to suit the parents. These were Lo Shu 3 and Lo Shu 4, corresponding to East and South-east. Both these numbers symbolised Wood. The huge amount of Wood was clashing badly with the child's Earth element, thus causing him severe illness. The Feng Shui Master advised the parents to move their West group child, to a room west of the parents room. In this case the parents had their bedroom in sector 1 (Kan). So the child was transferred to sector 6 (Chien) which was west of the parents room. The child recovered soon thereafter.

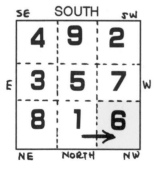

Sketch shows the child's new room that lies west of his parents room.

LESSON TO BE LEARNT:
Sometimes all that may be required to solve a Feng Shui problem is just to change rooms.

CASE 8: MOTHER/DAUGHTER RELATIONSHIP
Using Feng Shui directions to overcome incompatibilities

Shan Li's KUA number was 1, while her mother's was 8. She belonged to the East group and her mother belonged to the West group. In the Lo Shu Grid, Shan Li's number (1) coincided with her mother's Wu Kuei number. The two could not get along and neither could speak to the other without getting into a shouting match. The severity of the incompatibility was further compounded by the fact that, quite by chance, the oven's fire mouth was facing the northwest, (6 in the Lo Shu Grid). While this was good for the mother, it was an unfortunate situation for the daughter.

The Feng Shui Master advised moving Shan Li's bedroom to the southeast or No. 4 sector in the house. This corresponded to Shan Li's best direction and sector (Sheng Chi) and was therefore good for her. In addition, in that room she would be looking across at No.6 (the northwest sector) which coincided with her mother's "Tien Yi" number. Thus "Heaven came to cure the incompatibility". Mother and daughter now get along extremely well. More, Shan Li has achieved outstanding success in her studies.

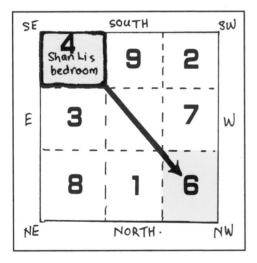

The sketch shows Shan Li's new bedroom where she is now in her "best" sector.

Looking across to the opposite direction, she is facing the northwest or No 6 sector.

This corresponds to her mother's Tien Yi (auspicious) position.

The relocation of her bedroom has cured the incompatibility between mother and daughter.

LESSON TO BE LEARNT:
The practitioner can use the Pa Kua Lo Shu system of Feng Shui to identify and overcome any incompatibilities between parents and their children.

CASE 9: THE MEDICAL STUDENT
Selecting the foreign university for your children

Gaik Lin, a brilliant student always wanted to be a doctor. After finishing her A levels with several distinctions, her parents had to decide whether to send her to a University in Australia, the U.K or elsewhere. Going to medical School was an expensive proposition and Gaik Lin knew that unless she obtained at least a part scholarship to help defray the expenses, the cost of her overseas studies would force her parents to make extensive sacrafices. Nevertheless, her parents wanted the very best University for her.

Gaik Lin's KUA No. was 7. This meant that her best directions were N.West, S.West, N.East, and West. The Feng Shui master advised her to go to Australia, since this meant that she would be travelling to her destination FROM the Northwest, thereby "bringing her best luck with her". If she were to choose the UK, the Master said, she would be travelling from the S.East which was "Lui Sha" direction, the direction of "six killings". The UK would be very inauspicious for her. gaik Lin took his advice and enrolled at the University of NSW in Sydney. Six months after arrival, Gaik Lin won a full scholarship from the University. She has since graduated with First Class Honours.

The sketch shows the direction of travel to popular University destinations considered by parents for their children. In selecting the country, determine your child's KUA number and most auspicious directions. Make sure your child is travelling FROM his/her best directions, and not travelling TO their

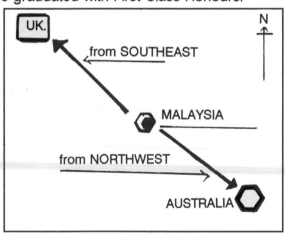

best directions. If they travel from their worst direction not only will they perform below expectations, but they might also fall ill or experience unfortunate situations. They will also not be very happy.

LESSON TO BE LEARNT:
When re-locating your children for further studies abroad, do select the destination which coincides with their best directions to ensure good fortune.

CASE 10: THE BUSINESS TRAVELLER
Using Feng Shui to route your travel plans

Edwin Tan travelled extensively in the course of his work as Director in charge of export markets for a large company making upmarket glassware. In this capacity he made regular trips to the United States and to Europe to participate in trade fairs and meet with foreign distributors and agents. He had been handling this job for nine months. At first, things went well after he took over from his predecessor. Recently however, he had been experiencing cancelled orders and problems from his foreign principals. The Managing Director had confided his concern and hinted that unless things improved, he would have to remove Edwin from the assignment. Edwin's KUA number was 8, and his best directions were S.West, N.West, West and N.East. The Feng Shui Master studied Edwin's Feng Shui Chart and shook his head. Travelling to Europe and then going from there to the United States meant Edwin was travelling FROM the S.East. This was his very worst direction, ie his Chueh Ming, a direction which signified "total destruction".

" But I must travel to these places, its my job !" he protested.
The Feng Shui Master advised him to calm down. "I have a solution" he offered, "one that will solve your problem."

The Master told Edwin to arrange his travel plans such that he would fly to the United States via Hong Kong, Tokyo and Los Angeles. This meant he would be flying FROM the S.West direction, his "Sheng Chi" direction (his most auspicious).

Going from the U.S. to Europe also meant he would be travelling FROM the West, again an auspicious direction for him. Since following the Feng Shui Master's advice Edwin has doubled export sales of his company within two years.

LESSON TO LEARN
When making important trips, make sure to travel FROM your lucky directions.

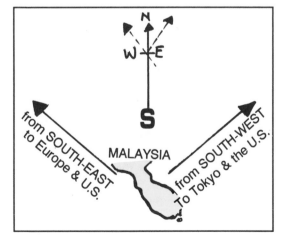

CASE 11: THE LARGE FAMILY
How to harness good directions for the whole family

A difficult dilemma facing the Feng Shui practitioner is how to arrange the orientation of the house in such a way as to benefit ALL members of the family. Fathers, Mothers and children have different KUA numbers, and consequently have different auspicious and inauspicious Lo Shu numbers and compass directions. Also, because of the way the formula works, what may be an excellent direction for one member of the family could very well be the worst direction for another. In such cases how does the Feng Shui Master decide ?

Mr Chen's family was a case in point. His KUA number was 2, and he belonged to the West group. His wife together with their three children all belonged to the East group. Thus his best direction, ie N.East represeneted varying degrees of bad luck for his whole family. This meant that if he oriented his Main door to suit himself, it would be inauspicious for everyone else.

In this particular instance the Feng Shui Master declared that he would keep the main door facing North East since Mr Chen was the breadwinner of the household. However he advised that the oven's fire mouth be utilised to serve both sets of occupants. There would thus be two rice cookers !

One would be positioned for Mr Chen. The fire mouth of his rice pot would face N.East, and he would eat rice cooked in this pot.
The other rice cooker would be oriented to have its source of electricity (its fire mouth) face East, a direction which would represent varying degrees of "good luck" for the rest of the family !

The sketch shows the two rice cookers facing different directions.

Mr Chen's Cooker facing North-East

Family Cooker facing East !

LESSON TO BE LEARNT
In Compass Direction Feng Shui, the fire mouth of the family cooker or oven, is an important consideration, which must not be ignored.

CASE 12: MR WANG'S ILLNESS
Activating the "Tien Yi" direction to cure an illness

Mr Wang became seriously ill shortly after having his kitchen renovated and modernised. The family started to worry when they realised he was not getting any better despite being treated by the best doctors. The strange thing was that the doctors could not find anything seriously wrong with him. Yet Mr Wang continued to be weak and feeble, constantly complaining of stomache pains and having frequent dizzy and fainting spells.

The Feng Shui Master was consulted. He checked the family rice cooker and discovered that it had its fire mouth facing south (or number 9). As Mr Wang's KUA number was 6, this was his Chueh Ming (or worst) direction. The Master quickly turned the cooker round such that its fire mouth was now facing north east, (number 8), which represented Mr Wang's Tien Yi (heavenly doctor) direction. Mr Wang recovered soon after.

Another similiar case was not so easily cured. Mr Wong's KUA number was also 6. As in the previous case, Mr Wong's oven had its fire mouth facing number 9, ie south. However, even after the fire mouth was changed to his Tien Yi direction, Mr Wong's illness persisted.

The Feng Shui Master then recommended he move to another house which was in his Tien Yi direction, ie N.East. After the move, Mr Wong soon recovered.

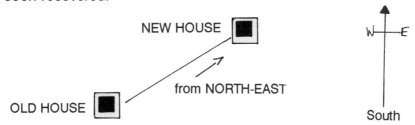

LESSONS TO BE LEARNT:
* The Tien Yi direction can be activated via the oven's fire mouth to cure persistent, regular or severe illnesses.

* Sometimes activating the oven mouth alone is insufficient. Location of dwelling is more potent as shown in the second case.

CASE 13: THE NEW HOUSE
Be aware of the direction of your move.

Their newly built house looked beautiful. Mrs Choo had been staying with her in laws in another town since her marriage to Chin Heng six years ago. She was excited about having her own house at last ! No more in laws ! Her husband had consulted a Feng Shui Master about the house and everything was perfect.

There was only one small detail. The Master had advised her husband that he should not move straight from his parents home into the new house. Instead, he suggested that Mr Choo should live for about six months in a sort of half way house which the Master had identified, and from there move into his new house. "It has to do with directions" the Master explained. Mrs Choo dismissed the recommendation as "absurd" and persuaded her husband to move straight into their new home, thus ignoring the Feng Shui Master's advice. Two months later Mr Choo died in an accident.

Mr Choo's KUA number was 2. His new house was South of his old house. He would thus be travelling from the North, his worst killing direction. He cannot stay in the new house yet. Instead he should first move to halfway house marked "A" (Northeast) or to the one marked "B" (Southwest).

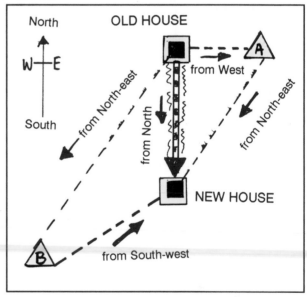

* To go to "A", he
  would first be travelling from West, and from there he would travel from Northeast. Both directions are auspicious.
* To go to "B" he would first be travelling from Northeast, and from there he would travel from Southwest, again both auspicious directions for him.

LESSON TO BE LEARNT:
When moving to a new house, bring good luck to your new place.

CASE 14: THE BUSINESS PARTNER
Evaluating compatability of partners

Siew Kim, Angela and Marina were partners in a florist shop. Siew Kim was a retired schoolteacher who had a talent for flower arrangement; Angela was a businesswoman with good organisational skills while Marina had excellent contacts and could bring in the customers. The partnership got off to a great start and within three months the shop was thriving. Plans were made to open a second store in another part of town. However, problems and disagreements soon developed in the partnership. The women differed over pricing and amount of flowers to stock. Deliveries suffered. Collections were slow and it wasn't long before the partnership ran out of cash. Disagreements developed into outright hostility with each accusing the other of over spending and giving of discounts to friends. Angela and Marina were no longer on speaking terms. It was clear by the fifth month the business was in serious trouble. Fed up with the constant bickering, Siew Kim proposed selling out to try and recoup at least some of the capital they had each put in. The decision was against her better judgement. Despite their problems she knew their shop could have been very successful.

Siew Kim decided to consult a Feng Shui Master, who decided to investigate the compatibility of the three partners using their respective KUA and Lo Shu numbers.

Siew Kim (KUA No.6) and Angela (KUA No. 8) both belonged to the West Group. Marina's KUA number was 4, and this corresponded to Angela's Chueh Ming (worst) Lo Shu number. It was not surprising that the partnership had failed. The respective numbers of the partners indicated a severe lack of incompatibility between Angela and Marina, whose KUA number was also Siew Kim's Ho Hai (bad luck) number. Though less severe in the incompatibility tables, the Marina/Siew Kim alliance was also fraught with difficulty. The charts however showed excellent potential for a fruitful partnership between Siew Kim and Angela, with each corresponding to the other's Tien Yi (auspicious) number. The Master advised them both to buy out Marina and start afresh. The partnership soon prospered.

LESSON TO BE LEARNT:
Remember that the Pa Kua Lo Shu system can be used to examine the compatability of partners, employees & associates.

CASE 15: THE HOUSE RENOVATION
Activating further good luck with repair work & renovations

Mr. Mah's good friend, Master Yap, was a Feng Shui Master of considerable repute. In the early years of their friendship Master Yap had helped design Mr Mah's house, and in the ensueing years Mr Mah's business had prospered. He was now a wealthy man, with two successful sons, one a doctor and another an accountant. He also had a relatively harmonious family life. *He was wary of making any changes to his house, since its Feng Shui had obviously served his family well, but Mr Mah badly wanted to update the doors and windows of his house, and also have a new set of interiors and furniture designed.* He was thus pleasantly surprised when, on consulting the Feng Shui Master, Mr Yap congratulated them. "Proceed," he smiled, "you can activate your luck with repair work ... repair the beams, change the tiles, repaint the windows, redesign the doors, improve your drainage.... extend the house, do anything you like ... and if the changes are made inside your auspicious Lo Shu locations it will be even better ... in fact do some work inside your best location and plenty big money will come your way ! "

Relieved, Mr Mah proceeded to bring in the architect and the interior decorator. Just before the workers moved in however, Mr Mah received a call from his Feng Shui friend, "Have you selected a suitable date to start work on your house ?". Of course he had not !

The Chinese often consult the Tong Shu to select a suitable date for starting work on constructions. But this is a generalised version. The Pa Kua system using the Lo Shu numbers of individuals select dates on the basis of the KUA elements. Thus, Mr Mah's KUA Number was 4. His best direction was North. His main door therefore faced North. This coincides with the Trigram Kan whose element symbol is Water. Mr Mah's renovations work cannot start on a Wood day, as Wood absorbs the Water; he also cannot commence work on an Earth day since Earth destroys or overcomes Water.

Mr Mah must therefore start work on either a Fire or a Metal day. To find out the elements of each of the days, just refer to a Chinese daily calendar.

LESSON TO BE LEARNT:
Good Feng Shui can be expanded with repair work, but when undertaking such repair work or renovation, make sure to start work on a suitable date.

CHAPTER SIX

FENG SHUI DIMENSIONS

AUSPICIOUS
DIMENSIONS for YANG DWELLINGS

Veteran practitioners of Feng Shui almost always use special Feng Shui dimensions when deciding on size of doors and windows, desks and tables and on all major pieces of furniture in the household and office. The author was given a custom made "Measuring Tape" some years ago which has measurements on one side of the tape (in cms and inches) and special markings on the other side of the tape.

These special markings specified the auspicious and inauspicious dimensions for two types of dwellings viz Yang dwellings (homes of the living) and Yin dwellings (homes of the dead ie coffins and gravesites).

What is presented here are the markings and dimensions for Yang dwellings.

Attempts to verify the origins of these Feng Shui dimensions have only been partially successful in that although Masters of Feng Shui freely acknowledged the existence and importance of lucky and unlucky dimensions, none could offer detailed information pertaining to the source of the measurements.

According to Master Yap Cheng Hai, who, like most of the Masters in Hong Kong, freely incorporates the use of Feng Shui measurements into his recommendations, these dimensions were first "discovered" by an Imperial carpenter of the Sung Dynasty, who incorporated them in his work for the emperor's family at the Imperial Palace. These dimensions were compiled and recorded for posterity, and seem to have survived intact to the present day.

Today Feng Shui dimensions are widely used in the design of office tables. The practice is particularly prevalent in Hong Kong, where elaborate rosewood tables with dragon designs are made according to Feng Shui dimensions.

THE AUSPICIOUS DIMENSIONS

For "Yang dwellings", there are eight cycles of dimensions in the Feng Shui Measuring Tape; four of these are generally auspicious and four are inauspicious.

The Tape measures the equivalent of 17 inches or 43cms which are then categorised into eight sections. After the eighth section, the Cycle of dimensions repeats itself. Thus the practitioner should work in cycles of 17 inches.

The Auspicious Dimensions are the first, fourth, fifth and eighth Section. Each of these sections has a name which describes it's lucky attributes.

THE FIRST SECTION, called CHAI (Lucky Dimension) is between 0 to 2 and 1/8 inches or 0 to 5.4 cms. This first CHAI is divided into four sub-categories of good luck. The first approximate 1/2 inch brings money luck; the second half inch brings a "safe filled with jewels" ; the next approximate half inch bring together six types of good luck, while the last section brings "abundant good fortune".

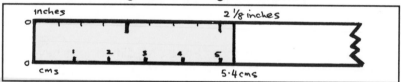

CHAI: the first Auspicious Section

THE FOURTH SECTION named YI lies between 6 and 3/8 inches to 8 and 1/2 inches; or 16.2 cms to 21.5 cms. This is a section which brings Mentor Luck ie the luck of helpful people. Once again there are four sub-sections. The first approximate half-inch means "blessed with many good children". The second approximate half inch predicts "added income from unexpected sources". The third approximate half-inch means" a very successful son", while the final approximate half-inch offers " very good fortune".

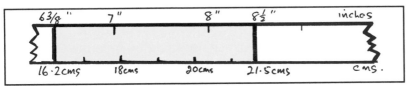

YI: the second Auspicious Section

THE FIFTH SECTION called KWAN (Power) continues on from the previous section and lies between 8 and 1/2 inches to 10 and 5/8 inches, or 21.5 cms to 27cms. This third auspicious set of dimensions also has four sub-sections, with the first approximate half inch meaning "easy to pass examinations successfully. The next approximate half-inch predicts "special luck" which generally refers to gambling or speculative luck, the kind that wins lotteries or four digit numbers ! The next approximate half-inch is called "improved income" while the final sub-section offers "prosperity, power and high honour for the family".

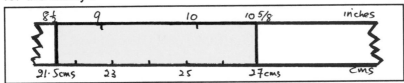

KWAN: the third Auspicious Section

THE EIGHTH SECTION, called PUN (meaning Capital) lies between 14 and 6/8 inches to 17 inches, or 37 and 1/2 cms to 43.2 cms. This is the fourth auspicious set of dimensions. Its first sub-category of good luck means "lots of money flowing in"; the next approximate half-inch spells "good luck in examinations". The third sub-category predicts plenty of jewellery, treasures and precious stones while the final sub-category offers "abundant prosperity and good fortune".

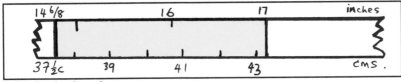

PUN: the fourth Auspicious section

These four auspicious sets of dimensions are repeated, by joining the sum total of all eight sections (good as well as bad) together so that continious sets of auspicious dimensions can be determined. This is illustrated in the Tape Measure here.

The auspicious sets of dimensions are repeated here (the shaded sections marked A, B, C and D) over two cycles. The non shaded sub-sections describe the unlucky dimensions, and these too have been repeated over two cycles.

The "good luck" sets of dimensions are summarised here for easy reference. Readers who are dealing with larger dimension furniture should make their calculations based on the method indicated here. The same principle of "extending" the auspicious sets of dimensions also apply to the unlucky dimensions.

SUMMARY OF THE GOOD LUCK DIMENSIONS:

CHAI: Between 0 inches and 2 and 1/8 inches
  : Between 17 inches and 19 and 1/8 inches
  : Between 34 inches and 36 and 1/8 inches
  : Between 51 inches and 53 and 1/8 inches

YI : Between 6 and 3/8 inches to 8 and 1/2 inches
  : Between 23 and 3/8 inches to 25 and 1/2 inches
  : Between 40 and 3/8 inches to 42 and 1/2 inches
  : Between 57 and 3/8 inches to 59 and 1/2 inches

KWAN: Between 8 and 1/2 inches to 10 and 5/8 inches
  : Between 25 and 1/2 inches to 27 and 5/8 inches
  : Between 42 and 1/2 inches to 44 and 5/8 inches
  : Between 59 and 1/2 inches to 61 and 5/8 inches

PUN : Between 14 and 6/8 inches to 17 inches
  : Between 31 and 6/8 inches to 34 inches
  : Between 48 and 6/8 inches to 51 inches
  : Between 65 and 6/8 inches to 68 inches

THE UNLUCKY DIMENSIONS

From the above discussion it should be obvious that the in-auspicious dimensions are those which do not fall between the good luck sections in our 17 inch cycle. For ease of reference however these bad luck dimensions are presented here together with their "meanings". As with the good luck sections, there are also different types of bad luck, some more severe than others. Readers should use these meanings as approximate indications.

The bad luck dimensions fall within the second, third, sixth and seventh sections of the 17 inch tape. These are named PI, LI, CHIEH and HAI respectively, and as in the previous case, the way to calculate the "larger" bad luck dimensions is to extend them by adding the cyclical 17 inches to the fundamental dimensions given.

THE SECOND SECTION called PI (means Sickness) lies between 2 and 1/8 inches to 4 and 2/8 inches or 5.4 cms to 10.8 cms. There are four sub sections in this first inauspicious section of the Tape, with the first approximate half-inch of this section carrying the meaning "Money Retreats". The next half-inch says there will be legal or Government related problems, or trouble with the authorities. The third approximate half-inch spells serious trouble because it means bad luck to the extent of "going to jail", while the final sub-category indicates the death of the spouse, thus leaving one widowed.

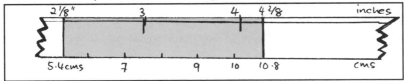

PI: the first Inauspicious section

THE THIRD SECTION named LI (meaning Separation) lies between 4 and 2/8 inches to 6 and 3/8 inches or between 10.8 cms to 16.2 cms. The four sub sections of bad luck here spell various situations of loss.

Thus the first approximate half-inch means "a store of bad luck", while the next half-inch means losing money or having money taken away from you. The third sub-section indicates meeting up with unscrupulous people who will cheat you while the fourth sub section predicts "everything will be lost or stolen".

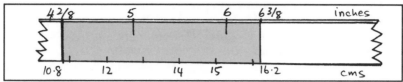

LI: the second Inauspicious section

THE SIXTH SECTION named CHIEH (Bad) is defined by the measurements 10 and 5/8 inches to 12 and 6/8 inches or between 27.0 cms to 32.4 cms. The meanings of this section indicate firstly a death and departure of some kind, next that everything you need will disappear and you will have your livelihood taken away from you.

The third sub-section indicates that you could be "chased out of your village in disgrace", while the fourth section indicates a very severe loss of money.

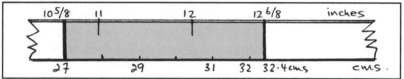

CHIEH: the third Inauspicious section

THE SEVENTH SECTION called HAI (getting Hurt) lies between 12 and 6/8 inches to 14 and 6/8 inches or between 32.4cms to 37.5 cms.

The four sub-categories signify severe bad luck starting with the first sub-category which means "Disasters come!". The second half-inch indicates death, while the third sub category predicts "sickness and ill health".
The last sub-category of bad luck here means "scandal and quarrels".

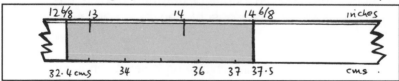

HAI: the fourth Inauspicious section

SUMMARY OF BAD LUCK DIMENSIONS

PI   : Between 2 and 1/8 inches to 4 and 2/8 inches
     : Between 19 and 1/8 inches to 21 and 2/8 inches
     : Between 36 and 1/8 inches to 38 and 2/8 inches
     : Between 53 and 1/8 inches to 55 and 2/8 inches

LI   : Between 4 and 2/8 inches to 6 and 3/8 inches
     : Between 21 and 2/8 inches to 23 and 3/8 inches
     : Between 38 and 2/8 inches to 40 and 3/8 inches
     : Between 55 and 2/8 inches to 57 and 3/8 inches

CHIEH: Between 10 and 5/8 inches to 12 and 6/8 inches
     : Between 21 and 5/8 inches to 29 and 6/8 inches
     : Between 38 and 5/8 inches to 46 and 6/8 inches
     : Between 55 and 5/8 inches to 63 and 6/8 inches

HAI : Between 12 and 6/8 inches to 14 and 6/8 inches
     : Between 29 and 6/8 inches to 31 and 6/8 inches
     : Between 46 and 6/8 inches to 48 and 6/8 inches
     : Between 63 and 6/8 inches to 65 and 6/8 inches

HOW TO USE THE FENG SHUI DIMENSIONS

THE WORKING DESK AND TABLE

This piece of furniture, either at the office or at home, is the most obvious application of the Dimension technique. Basically, the table top should have both the length and the breadth be designed according to Feng Shui dimensions.

Where large desks have an adjoining piece (very common in modern offices) attached to the main desk forming an "L" shape, the advice is to sever the connection since this is not an auspicious shape. Far better to have two tables both made with lucky dimensions.

The height of the desk or table is extremely important. This definately must follow Feng Shui dimensions, even if it means having the table slightly too high for comfort. The solution is often to "raise" the chair in the case of shorter people (or women executives) by making a special platform which is placed under the chair.

Shown here are three examples of executive desks which have been designed and constructed with good dimensions. For those who are particularly fussy, the dimensions of drawers and shelves inside the desks may also be made to follow good dimensions, although this is not a vital aspect of the practice. Most important is basically to ensure that the length, breadth and height are auspicious.

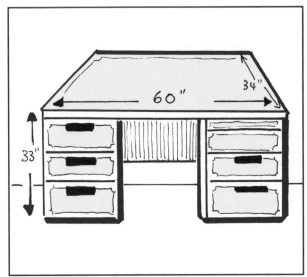

An imposing Director's Desk

* From the dimensions given the reader may check their meanings to see whether the kind of luck indicated is what is wished for. Otherwise the dimension should be modified to more accurately reflect one's wishes. * Parents, when designing desks for their children can attempt to "tap" the examination luck indicated in the dimensions.*

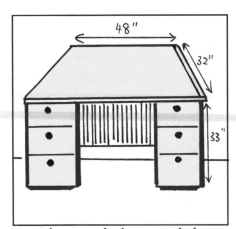

A medium sized Manager's desk

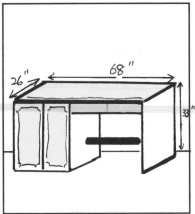

A secretary's table

THE BED & BEDROOM FURNITURE

While most modern western style beds are of "standard dimensions", ie being singles, doubles, queen-size or king-size, it is possible to vary the height of the bed according to Feng Shui dimensions. Beds are important in the Feng Shui context because it symbolises a place of rest. Similiarly the other pieces of bedroom furniture can also be customised with Feng Shui dimensions factored in. This refers to dressing tables, chairs, book cases, bedside tables and linen boxes.

Where possible, it is advisable to ensure that book-shelves built in the bedroom should not be either just behind the bed or on walls surrounding the bed. Exposed bookshelves can sometimes symbolise fierce poison arrows pointed at the sleeping figure on the bed. Hence shelves should be at low levels, and preferably be within the auspicious dimensions spelt out in the earlier section.

Where there are mirrors attached to dressing tables these should preferably be sited such that the the mirror does NOT face the bed at all. Feng Shui Masters warn that waking up to one's own image in the mirror can be a "jolting" experience. Others also maintain that mirror surfaces which are visible from the bed can often lead to discord between husband and wife. For this reason most Feng Shui Masters do not encourage having mirrors incorporated into the decor of the bedroom.

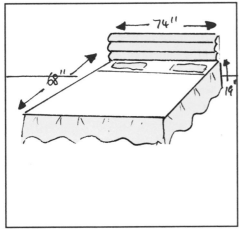

Bed Dimensions

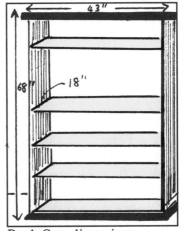

Book-Case dimensions

CUPBOARDS & BOOK-SHELVES

When designing built-ins for the house or office, it is often advisable to follow the Feng Shui dimensions given, adjusting the size accordingly. This is specifically recommended for the shelves in the study, the display cupboards and the kitchen cabinets.

Those who are more meticulous can also follow the "meanings" given for each of the auspicious "dimension-sectors" in order to activate the various kinds of good fortune desired. While such fastidious application of Feng Shui precepts may seem far fetched, and even a trifling inconvenient, there are carpentars in town who are already well versed with these dimensions and they often are able to adjust measurements and proportions accordingly, once the "table of dimensions" are given to them.

DOORS & WINDOWS

These represent the entry and exit points of the home, where Chi flows in and out. As such, it is always advisable to build them not just according to auspicious directions, but also to lucky dimensions. This applies to both the length and width of the windows and doors, and in the case of windows, also to the height from the ground level.

The measurements used must be proportionate so that visually there is balance and harmony. Doors which are too large or too small in proportion to the overall size of the room, or the house, are strongly discouraged since this suggests an imbalance of some kind.

The practitioner is therefore advised to adjust the dimensions according to the "cycles", ie enlarging or contracting the size wherever necessary. Windows and Doors with semi-circle tops are acceptable from a Feng Shui view-point. It is not necessary to worry about the diameter of the semi-circle since the length and breadth of the window or door has already been properly measured.

Feng Shui stays nuetral on sliding glass doors for the home or office, although the author has been told by most Feng Shui Masters that the main door should be "solid" and strong, and preferably not be made of glass (which is "see-through"), or of louvred wood panels. A solid door represents strength and stability.

CHAPTER SEVEN

USING FENG SHUI TO IMPROVE YOUR LIFE

Within the modern day environment of the twentieth century, the wisdom of the ancients is oftentimes misconstrued as lacking in scientific justification. A certain amount of scepticism is thus inevitable especially among those who are unsure of the basis of so called "Feng Shui formulas", or those who do not understand much of the philosophical under-pinnings of the concepts of Feng Shui.

This kind of cynicism can often be so entrenched that Feng Shui is then dismissed as so much "hocus pocus" or "frivolous superstition". The existence of some charlatans in the Feng Shui consultancy business does not help either.

It is within such a context that the interested practitioner should educate himself or herself with the "basics" of Feng Shui before consulting a Feng Shui man. This leads to greater depth of understanding and appreciation of the recommendations offered and/or changes proposed.
Sometimes such consultation may even be unnecessary once the broad outlines of the "do's and dont's" and the reasons behind these "rules" are fully understood.

If Feng Shui is regarded as a science of some kind - its laws promulgated and compiled on the basis of hundreds of years' worth of observed quantitative data, then understanding and practising Feng Shui can become an activity of great fascination and reward.

The author is convinced that there is a great deal of substantive value in Feng Shui practice, and this conviction is based not only on years of personal experience but also from serious study and observation of the way Feng Shui works, especially when the two major schools of practise ie the Landscape or Form School and the Compass School are merged.

It is indeed possible to use Feng Shui to improve the quality of one's life. Bad luck can be "modified" to take on less serious consequences, while good luck can be enhanced and magnified. Specific areas of one's life can be enriched and problems of every nature can be overcome.

This raises the question, " Can one's destiny be changed ? ".

If it can, and if good Feng Shui practice is the key to this change, then does it not imply that fortune telling and all related divination sciences are not totally reliable indicators of one's fate and destiny ?

How does one then explain the parallel existence of beliefs in the powers of divination accorded to Chinese Astrology, the Ganzhi System, and even the I-Ching, the so called "source-book" of both Feng Shui and the fore-casting practices of the Chinese ?

Ancient Chinese Classics and Texts abound with categorical statements that address this issue directly. According to these Texts, Destiny can be changed if one possesses the keys (or the know-how) to effect such change. Gaining a knowledge of the keys to unlock the secrets, say these Texts, requires an understanding of the workings of the Universe and Man's relationship with his environment.

Through the ages ie every few hundred years, a wise man emerges who adds on to this knowledge, offering Commentaries, Judgements and Interpretations, and leaving behind a rich heritage of knowledge for further study and enhancement by subsequent generations. Such a man was of course the great thinker and philosopher, Confucius whose contributions in these areas is legendary.

Against this vast tapestry of knowledge, Master Practitioners have extracted the essence of the body of knowledge required to practice effective Feng Shui as well as effective Fortune- Telling. These two branches of the body of metaphysical knowledge which has been passed down to modern day practitioners do not therefore necessarily conflict so much as complement each other.

Indeed Compass School Feng Shui, which uses the horoscope or birth chart of a person to determine the way his/her house should be aligned and oriented, pointedly combines these two branches of practice.

Which is why there is often an element of divination and prediction in Feng Shui practice.

On December 24th 1992, the Asian Wall Street Journal carried a very interesting front page story on Feng Shui.

"A kind of Crystal Ball", it labelled Credit Lyonnais's "Feng Shui Index", an index which had tracked the major turning points of the Hong Kong Stock market's Hang Seng Index 12 months in advance. The Journal reported that stock market analysts working at the Hong Kong arm of Credit Lyonnais Securities had consulted a trio of "Feng Shui" experts on what they thought of Hong Kong Stocks in the year of the Monkey (1992). These experts used a combination of astrological and geographical calculations to measure and redress the imbalances of Hong Kong's natural and man made environment, to put together the Feng Shui index for the local stock market for the Lunar year which began in February 1992.

By December of that year, it had become clear to the analysts that this same Feng Shui Index was "an almost perfect map of the market's turning points".

Spurred on by this incredible performance which received widespread publicity, Credit Lyonnais commissioned a similiar index for 1993 - the year of the Rooster.

The Feng Shui team of experts obligingly complied with an Index for 1993 (interested stock market punters who follow the Hong Kong market may write direct to Credit Lyonnais in Hong Kong for a copy of the 1993 index !!), and with a few predictions for the rest of the year thrown in for good measure. (An important leader will die in April or May; politicians in Taiwan will be sick. Hong Kong will see more voilence ...)

It is necessary to understand that these are NOT tabloid predictions.

These are prophecies offered by Feng Shui experts of the colony. Granted that to the untrained person, Feng Shui analysis of this kind could very well sound like, "bulletins from a psychedelic zoo", since so much of the explanation describe the inter-actions of the twelve animals of the Chinese Zodiac, and in turn, their inter-actions with the five Elements.

In fact, the detailed explanations offered by the Feng Shui experts, as they described these inter-actions from month to month and then offered interpretations in terms of stock market performance, sounded "a bit like technical analysis".

According to the projects head at the securities firm, the Feng Shui men's analysis can very easily be compared to the mathematical market forecasting methods widely used on Wall Street.

Stories such as this recent one compels the well seasoned professional to walk the fine line between skepticism and disbelief on one hand and boyish excitement on the other. Indeed, skip over to the Phillipines for an even more dramatic tale of Feng Shui.

On the 4th January 1993, the New Straits Times of Malaysia carried the headline "Ramos to heed Geomancy advice", and proceeded to repeat a Reuter's narrative that President Fidel Ramos had said he would look into reports that three misplaced trees as well as unlucky symbols on the presidential seal and on the country's bank-notes were to blame for many of the misfortunes and natural calamities afflicting the Phillipines.

According to Chinese Feng Shui, the report stated, Ramos was told that these were the three major sources of bad luck in the country.

The three huge trees stood in front of the Malacanang Presidential Palace. These trees allegedly blocked the flow of cosmic energy, thereby preventing good fortune from coming to the President. Feng Shui experts suggested that these trees be cut down.

Mean-while the symbol of the sea-lion in the presidential seal had an inauspicious crooked tail, while the stars around it suggested darkness, signifying disasters.

Finally, the 500 peso bill was unlucky because it contained 13 stars, showed 13 people and the number 500 appeared 13 times !

In the light of latter day accounts such as the two reports highlighted here, Feng Shui seems to be enjoying a dramatic revival of interest. At least this is how it would appear to those whose exposure to its practice has been limited. To those of us who have studied Feng Shui for many years however, news of Feng Shui's apparent mysterious potency does not come as a surprise. In Hong Kong, local Chinese businessmen and stock market punters to whom consulting the Feng Shui man is normal business practice, the accuracy of the Feng Shui Index came as no surprise. To the Westerners (expatriates) based in the Colony however, the report appeared to be both incredible and unbelievable.

Master Yap Cheng Hai, one of the author's learned Feng Shui Masters, told Malaysia's TV Tiga's MONEYMATTERS program, "... so what is there to lose in believing in Feng Shui. If it does not work, all one has done is move around some furniture or changed a sitting position ... on the other hand if Feng Shui does work, the good luck is yours, not mine..."

USING FENG SHUI TO IMPROVE FAMILY LIFE.

One of the most appealing aspects of Feng Shui's potency is the way it can be harnessed to vastly improve family life. By this one refers not only to overall harmony within the family, but also it can be used to correct potentially tragic situations.

Thus, there are special Feng Shui orientations which can be activated:

* *to produce sons (or children) to childless couples;*
* *to increase affections between husband and wife:*
* *to reduce areas of friction between members of a family:*
* *to entice home a wayward son or daughter;*
* *to entice home a wayward husband or wife;*
* *to bring about a marriage or a birth in the family;*
* *to improve the health of any sickly member of the family:*
* *to effect reconciliations between quarrelling members of the family:*

There are formulas for activating all and each of the "family happiness" situations mentioned. These involve the use of the Lo-Shu numbers and the compass direction orientations contained in the Formula given in Chapters Three and Four. The Lo-Shu numbers that correspond to the Nien Yen position and directions are the most effective in creating family type "happiness" situations. Thus depending on which member of the family is affected and depending on what aspect of the situation is to be activated, the practitioner can make changes to the sleeping position or to the direction of the oven-mouth. Or changes can be made to room locations of the children who appear to be creating "problems" for the family.

If there are problems relating to the health of any member of the family, then it is the Tien Yi number(s) which should be activated. Tien Yi is conducive to bringing about the return to health of ailing children or sick people. Once again it is the sleeping position or the direction of the oven mouth which could be altered.

One very difficult problem which afflict modern day families is the appearance sometimes of a third party from outside who threatens to break up the family. This is the case when a successful husband and father begins to "stray" when he becomes the target of an aggressive female. Usually a situation like this would never arise if the Feng Shui of the house had been oriented correctly in the first place, particularly the location of the bedroom and/or the sleeping direction of the husband and wife. Some Feng Shui masters also maintain that having a pool located on the right side of the Main door (ie the direction when taken from inside the house) causes the man of the house to have several "wives". In such cases suitable Feng Shui changes should be made to address this specific problem.

Another common problem facing families pertains to way-ward or disobedient children; or to juveniles who have a hard time taking their school work seriously. Such children often mix with unsuitable peer groups or indulge in other anti-establishment type behaviour. Provided that the problem is genuine, once again Feng Shui can often "cure' the situation. The recommendation given in such cases is to activate the child's Nien Yen direction (which will bring him/her closer to the family); or to activate his Sheng Chi direction (which will make him mores serious in his work). Often, if the Sheng Chi can be effectively tapped by changing the sleeping and sitting directions, a change can be seen and felt quite speedily.

If changes are not noticed, the Text recommends that additional analysis be undertaken with the objective of making further use of the Pa-Kua Lo-Shu formula by using it on other applications.

USING FENG SHUI TO IMPROVE BUSINESS

Probably the most popular application of Feng Shui concepts occur within the business community. In Hong Kong, Singapore and Taiwan, the Feng Shui man is almost always consulted when new business premises - buildings, offices, factories, warehouses, property projects, condominium developments, shopping complexes - are built. Because there is such a high demand for their services, Feng Shui Consultants in these three countries do a roaring trade.

The Feng Shui that is practised is usually a combination of the Form School and the Compass School, and as such, Green Dragon White Tiger formations are incorporated against a background of special compass calculations, to ensure abundant good fortune and continious good profits for the businesses.

Pa-Kua Lo-Shu Formulations are extremely useful for Business Feng Shui. They are also easy to use, since the formulas can be employed by every person within a business organisation to improve his/her Feng Shui, sometimes just by re-orientating the sitting direction alone. Generally it is the Chief Executive's office and sitting position which has the greatest impact on the success or failure of the business. However where Feng Shui is practised by the entire chain of command within a management organisation structure then the potential for good fortune is considerably enhanced.

FENG SHUI FOR BRANCH NETWORKS
This approach is especially useful in retail or consumer type businesses which have a branch network throughout the country and therefore have a group of branch managers. Examples of these types of businesses are banks, finance companies, insurance companies, restaurants, fast-food outlets and other retail chain stores, department stores, supermarkets, convenience stores, and other specialised boutique type chain stores.

If every branch manager's Feng Shui were correctly oriented, ie with the main door facing the correct direction; with the branch manager's office properly aligned to his/her birth chart; with his/her sitting position facing the respective best (Sheng Chi) directions; and with other Feng Shui rules observed, the overall effect will be excellent and smooth progress of the company's plans. Companies which practise Feng Shui in this way usually do very well.

FENG SHUI AT THE HEAD OFFICE

If the network's Feng Shui were also complemented by excellent Feng Shui at head office level as well, ie whereby the Chief Executive (or general manager)'s desk, his/her sitting position as well as the front door to the office are aligned correctly to tap maximum Chi flows, truly abundant good fortune will definately flow into the company.

The practice of office Feng Shui to enhance profitability is often supplemented with the active addition of "Feng Shui" catalysts such as installing an aquarium, or having a minature fountain, or using bamboo flutes, wind-chimes and crystals.

The use of these catalysts is extensively covered in the author's introductory first book on Feng Shui. Much of the recommendations in this area of Feng Shui came from Hong Kong Masters who often had to enhance business Feng Shui merely by improving alignments, directions and locations at offices located within high rise buildings. As such a great deal of creativity was used to interpret and adapt classical Feng Shui concepts for the modern day office environment.

Companies which are involved in a good amount of trading activities, eg stock-broking firms, the money market and foreign exchange departments of banks, commodity broking firms and other similiar market oriented businesses are generally advised to pay special attention to the Feng Shui of their dealing rooms, not only with the intention of enhancing profits from their daily trades, but more important, to safeguard against heavy losses within a very volatile business.

The author is personally acquainted with at least two stockbroking firms in Hong Kong, where the dealing tables and chairs were made according to Feng Shui dimensions, and the direction of computer terminals as well as telephone sockets were all aligned in accordance with the birth chart of the chief and section-head dealers.

Quite a number of the treasury operations of banks in Hong Kong have also benefited from the close attention given to Feng Shui. Dealing profits are then maintained at respectable levels, and major losses are NOT recorded. Those familiar with financial dealing rooms will vouch for the fact that because financial, capital, money and forex markets are so volatile these days, it is extremely easy to make costly mistakes in the course of a day's trading.

In Malaysia, one of the country's most successful securities trading firm ordered special tables for their dealers and remisiers from the first day of operations. This was to ensure good profits and turnover for the company. In addition the direction of the firm's two executive directors were also carefully aligned. Today this same firm runs a billion dollar book and has been one of the most consistently profitable securities company in Kuala Lumpur.

In recent years, property developers have also begun paying close attention to the Feng Shui aspects of their condominium and housing projects. They realise that taking the trouble to ensure good Feng Shui for their projects usually translate into high turnover, and also assures families who move in to the new housing estate or condominium a generally smooth, lucky and happy environment.

As a result of this new awareness, Feng Shui Masters (from Singapore & Hong Kong) are generally consulted during the planning stages. The specific "Feng Shui" attributes of the developments are also incorporated into sales advertisements. Some companies even offer new buyers "free consultation" from in house "Feng Shui" experts !

Commercial buildings which have been pre-scrutinised by Feng Shui experts and who have incorporated correct lucky features into the buildings often find little difficulty in attracting tenants, who in turn are happy to pay their rents promptly because their businesses, located in those buildings enjoy good profitability.

Generally, in such buildings, where good landscape or form school Feng Shui features have already been incorporated, it is doubly beneficial to then align personal directions correctly since the effect will be even more powerful. This is done by determining the Lo-Shu numbers and directions that best align the business to its environment.

Where Compass School methods are utilised, the practitioner may use the date of incorporation of a company as its "date of birth".
It is also acceptable to use the date of birth of the company's owner (in the case of sole proprietorships) or of the company's chief executive (in the case of a public company or a partnership).
Often, the incorporation of Element analysis can also be very effective in tapping good Chi flows. This ensures that there is excellent harmony within the business environment.

USING FENG SHUI
TO IMPROVE CAREER PROSPECTS

Feng Shui holds truly exciting promise for the individual practitioner.

Upwardly mobile career professionals, who wish to consider using Feng Shui to improve their carrers should look on the exercise as acquiring extra knowledge to use as a supplementary asset. Possessing such an inclination, accompanied by a determination to understand the complex concepts that lie behind Feng Shui practice will lead those who undertake this study seriously to a fascinating and rewarding conclusion.

Usually this means being fairly single minded about checking every aspect of both schools of Feng Shui, ie first the Form school to ensure that the environment and the surrounding landscape is generally in harmony with the house (place of residence) and the office (place of work); it is also to ensure that no poison arrows are pointed at main doors and entrances.

Landscape Feng Shui revolves around the Cosmic breath, ie Chi, and understanding this thoroughly opens up new dimensions of Man's relationships with the environment, a view of the Universe according to the ancient Chinese texts. Such an understanding makes the practice of Feng Shui much easier.

Once this background of Feng Shui is firmly understood, studying the influence of the Pa-Kua and the Lo-Shu magic square on Compass directions will reveal exciting possibilities. Indeed this method of applying Feng Shui formulations is ideally suited to the individual since many of the practical aspects of the method are so easy to put to the test.

At this stage, it is perhaps relevant to reiterate that since Feng Shui is neither a religion, nor magical hocus pocus, the question of faith does not enter the picture. The author has always approached the practice of Feng Shui as a science, albeit a science which is as yet not fully understood. A certain amount of "testing" is therefore not taboo.
Over the years it has become obvious that Feng Shui does produce results of a sometimes spectacular nature. In the year the author changed her desk dimensions and her office directions to match those of her Lo-Shu numbers, she was "promoted" three times.

It is therefore with a certain amount of confidence that she can strongly recommend that for those who wish to use Feng Shui to improve their career and promotion prospects, they should undertake the following:

1. *CHECK THE OFFICE:*

* Check the main entrance to the office. Is it in your best (Sheng Chi) direction ? If so it is excellent. If not, is it in any of your other good directions ? If it is, good. If it is not and you can do something about it, change the direction to favour you. If you cannot, is there another door you can use to get in and out of the office which is facing one of your good directions ?

* Check the entrance to your own office/room. Follow the same routine as above. Ideally you should enter your own office from your Sheng Chi direction.

* Check the LOCATION of your room vis-a-vis the whole office. Is it in the most auspicious of your four locations ? If so excellent, if not can you do something about it ?

* Check the LOCATION of your desk/table within your room. Is the table placed in such a way that you do not have your back to the door ? Are you sitting facing you best DIRECTION ? If so it is excellent. If not, do move your table around such that you are facing at least one of your best directions. Do remember that you should not have your back to the door, or to the window. There should be a solid wall behind you to provide "support".

* Check the dimensions of your table/desk. Make sure the length, breadth and height of your table conform to the Feng Shui dimensions given in Chapter Six. Getting your dimensions correctly measured will activate good Feng Shui luck.

* Check that other pieces of furniture (whether movable or built in) in the room do not have edges pointed at you. That bookshelves do not represent sharp edges pointed at you. If there are any "threatening" pieces of furniture, move them round or get rid of them.

* Check that you are not sitting under an overhanging beam. Move your chair/table out of the way if you are underneath it. Exposed

beams cause headaches and a disturbed mind which clouds your judgement. Sometimes the presence of overhanging beams can be extremely severe in multi-storey high rise offices. This is especially so in the case of structural beams because these are normally repeated, ie one on top of the other on every floor. Can you imagine the "weight" of these mulitiple beams pressing on you ? Nothing you do can alleviate the heaviness of such structural beams. The only thing to do is to make sure you do not sit under a beam like that.

* Check that there are no protruding columns from corners which are pointed at you. If there are, use plants to camouflage and deflect the bad Chi coming from the corner.

* Finally use some Feng Shui activators like hanging a wind-chime, a crystal ball or installing a small fish tank. A word of warning ! Do not overdo it !! Remember that Feng Shui is all about harmony and balance. Do not make the mistake a friend of the author made. When told that an aquarium would be good for him, this erstwhile gentlemen greedily installed a huge oversize aquarium which took up one third of his room. The large amount of water dominated his office, and it also clashed badly with his element. Within six months he had been asked to "resign" from his high powered job with the company.
In the practice of Feng Shui more is not always better !!

2. CHECK THE HOME

* Check the main entrance door to your home. Make sure it is in your Sheng Chi direction. If it is not make sure it is at least in one of your four auspicious directions. The main door of your home is especially important since this has an important impact on your career.

* Check your study and the working desk in your study. If you do not have such a room then check the direction of the desk within the house which you do use. It is also important to determine the LOCATION of your desk, and to ensure that it is in one of you four best locations.

* Check your kitchens and toilet locations. Make sure they are located in one of you four BAD locations. Any toilet located in one of your best directions should ideally not be used since it "flushes" away your opportunities. For this reason toilets are usually to be located in an inauspicious position.

* Check all dimensions of important pieces of furniture within the house itself. It is helpful if their measurements conform to Feng Shui dimensions.

* Check your bedroom location and your sleeping direction. To enjoy good career growth, opportunities must come your way and you must be able to tap these opportunities. The sleeping position has an important effect on this aspect. To create abundant career luck you MUST sleep with your head pointed towards your Sheng Chi direction. This is within your control and even though this could require you to sleep at an "angle", do so !!

The above checklist itemises important alignments which must be "right". Only start to refine the practice after you have undertaken enough work on both your office and your house. It is also important not to be too obsessed about Feng Shui. This is because while good Feng Shui helps, it is not an automatic "open sesame" to success.

According to the Chinese, good Feng Shui works by enhancing good luck and deflecting bad luck. Bad Feng Shui on the other hand attracts bad luck, and if you happen to be going through a "bad period", there is no solace, or escape from difficulties and problems encountered.

Career path upward mobility often depends on one's interpersonal interactions with the boss, and with your colleagues. Good Feng Shui ensures that there is harmony between you and the people you inter-act with. Difficult situations then tend to sort themselves out.

Generally speaking the Feng Shui of one's house is more important than the Feng Shui of one's office. If the sleeping position is correct and the main door of the home is correctly aligned, one's Feng Shui is generally deemed to be good.

USING FENG SHUI
TO IMPROVE STUDENT PERFORMANCE

The Chinese have always regarded education with a great deal of reverence. In the old days, passing the Imperial examinations was one of the surest way of making a quantum leap upwards in terms of social status and career advancement. Often, merely having a single brilliant son was sufficient to "pull" an entire family from a lower social strata to a higher one. Thus, much of the Chinese cultural definations of happiness or success always included "scholastic success" for the sons of the family.

Feng Shui Texts proclaim that good Feng Shui can often improve the scholastic performance of the children of the household, by aligning their rooms and sleeping positions according to their birth-charts.

Within the symbolisms of the Trigrams and the Pa-Kua, six of the "sides" of the Pa-Kua refer to the children of the family, three sons and three daughters. These symbolisms are used by certain schools of Feng Shui to pin point the best rooms (in terms of location) within a household for each of the children.

Pa-Kua Lo-Shu Feng Shui formulations are even more exact. According to this method, the children's horoscopes are used to determine their auspicious Lo-Shu numbers which in turn allows their most auspicious rooms, and their most auspicious directions within a house to be revealed. Once these indicators have been resolved, parents who wish to improve the Feng Shui of their children should:

* select the room in the house that is best suited for the child.
* align his/her bed such that his/her head is pointed in the Sheng Chi direction. (Or one of the other three auspicious directions).
* place his/her desk such that he/she is studying, or doing homework, while seated facing his/her best direction.

These three "changes" are the all important prime aspects to consider. Other Feng Shui factors can also be contemplated but the above three are the "basics" to get right.

Matters pertaining to main door directions and oven-mouth orientations should generally be in accordance with the father or mother's Lo-Shu numbers rather than those of the children.

It is also advisable to make a desk and chair for the student in accordance with dimensions that promote the achievement of excellence in examinations. Studying and doing homework and assignments on auspicious tables do help in improving performance.

According to Feng Shui Masters, getting the dimensions and the directions aligned in a way which results in the harmonious intermingling of the individual's Chi and the environment's Chi improves mental faculties and learning abilities.
Clearheadedness is then the result.

There is also another aspect of Feng Shui which can be consulted when parents are contemplating sending their children overseas for Higher Education. This involves the careful analysis of travel directions. Depending on the individual's Lo-Shu numbers, travelling in certain directions can be more auspicious. These directions MUST be checked out.

The method for determing auspicious directions of travel, as they pertain to business travel and re-location travel (as in the case of a transfer) has already been covered in earlier chapters.

The same method can also be used to determine whether, for instance, sending one's son to the United Kingdom will be more beneficial for him than say, Australia. Where a student is able to "tap" his best direction of travel, going abroad will bring excellent results and prospects.

Where the direction of travel corresponds to his worst (or other bad) direction(s), a great deal of problems and difficulties will be encountered, sometimes leading to poor performance or even worse.

Finally, for older students, another method of applying Pa-Kua Lo-Shu Feng Shui is to try and "sit" facing one's best directions when taking important examinations and when attending lectures. This is easily done once one is in possession of one's auspicious directions, since all it requires is to slightly shift one's direction of sitting. When it is not possible to tap the best direction, any of the other three auspicious directions will also be beneficial. Once again however it is important to reiterate that Feng Shui can only help. It cannot produce miraculously brilliant results. It can, however, ward off severe bad luck and contribute towards improved performance.

CHAPTER EIGHT

THE CHINESE HOROSCOPE

The inclusion of this chapter on traditional Chinese Horoscopes (or Astrology) in a book on Pa-Kua Lo-Shu Feng Shui is meant to emphasize the connections between these two branches of Chinese metaphysical cultural beliefs. Both Chinese Feng Shui and Chinese Astrology are based, to a very large extent, on the I-Ching, on the Ganzhi System and on the inter-actions of the five Elements.

Chinese Astrology describes the universal characteristics of individuals and countries in accordance with their dates of birth; Chinese Astrology also reveals general trends of "good" years and "bad" years.

When retained to advise a client, Feng Shui Masters often undertake at least a cursory analysis of his/her birth chart to determine whether the year in question is generally auspicious or not for the client.

They believe that if the year spells bad luck for the client, then the emphasis of the Feng Shui would be to try and "ward off" bad Chi which may be caused by poison arrows and other structures which create Sha Chi. The accent is thus on defensive measures which will allow the client to "tolerate" and survive a bad year before attempting to introduce more auspicious Feng Shui features later.

During a generally good year on the other hand, the emphasis of the Feng Shui Master will be to "tap" into the good luck already predicted by the Horoscope, in order to magnify the good fortune.

It has been emphasized to the author by several Masters that while the Destiny of Man can be changed by Feng Shui, this has to be done with a great deal of care. And of course, requires considerable expertise and experience. Feng Shui, it is stressed makes up only a third of a person's overall "luck".

Feng Shui is the luck harnessed from the Earth's Chi; while what is revealed through the Horoscopes shows the destiny bestowed by Heaven. For Earth luck (Ti Chai) to overcome Heaven luck (Tien Chai) requires not just the inputs of Man's own luck (Ren Chai), but also sufficient understanding of the "relative strength" of the Heaven Luck, ie the details of a person's Horsocope reading. For this reason, Feng Shui Masters are sometimes more succesful with some clients than with others.

Instances have also been pointed out to the author where even with the inputs of several Masters, whose combined expertise on Feng Shui can be inordinately impressive, some people "just cannot be helped, because they do not, at a particular time, have the luck to be helped, or whose bad period is in such adverse shape, the most that can be done is to reduce the ill effects of a particularly bad year".

An example of just such a case was narrated to the author by Master Yap. The incident occured in Kuala Lumpur many years ago. A very successful contractor had invited a highly respected old Master from Taiwan to design the Feng Shui of his new mansion in Pantai Hills. The Master studied his birth chart, and queitly shook his head. He nevertheless did what he could and before leaving Kuala Lumpur advised the contractor (and reminded him several times) not to make any additions or changes to the building plans.

Privately however, he confided to Master Yap Cheng Hai, who at that time was learning some aspects of Compass School Feng Shui from him, that he very much feared the contractor was headed for "severe troubles the following year".

The contractor's luck, the old Master predicted, would be so bad the next year that it would be very difficult to help him. True enough, after the old Master left, the contractor decided to add a huge swimming pool in the garden in place of a tiny fish pond suggested by the Master. The contractor had come to the conclusion that the pond was to signify the inflow of money, and instead of the trickle of money indicated by a tiny pond, he wished for a deluge of money which he believed would be symbolised by a pool.

He was also keen to have a swimming pool in the house because it was at that time quite the latest status symbol.

Alas, his reasoning had been shallow, and totally contradicted the old

Master's intentions. The tiny pond balanced the Chi harmony of the man's garden and home, and had been meant also to deflect some poisonous Chi created by the destructive interactions of Elements in the contractor's birthchart. Changing the pond into a large swimming pool completely destroyed his Feng Shui.

In the following year, soon after his house was built (being a contractor he built it in record time), the contractor was arrested under the ACA, and convicted for bribing a Govt official. His business also collapsed because of over extension in the property market, and he was declared a bankrupt !!

The practise of Feng Shui should therefore be supplemented with at least some knowledge of astrological influences. It is also important to understand that the laws of the Universe, according to the Chinese scheme of things is dynamic and constantly changing. One does not go against the forces and the energies of the Universe; during bad times, one bides one's time and stays patient. Bad times and bad fortune, according to the I Ching almost always lead to better times if one stays balanced with the forces of the Universe.

THE TWELVE ANIMAL SIGNS

Chinese Astrology is based on the lunar calendar, which dates back to the time of Emperor Huang Ti (about 2600 BC). It divides Time into 60 year cycles, made up of twelve years (that correspond to twelve Animal signs) and five Elements. Thus 12 x 5 makes 60 years.

According to legend, Twelve animals came to bid farewell to the Amitabha Buddha when he ascended to Heaven. These animals, in order of their arrival, were the Rat, the Ox, the Tiger, the Rabbit, the Dragon, the Snake, the Horse, the Sheep, the Monkey, the Rooster, the Dog and the Boar. To commemorate their presence at his ascension to heaven, Lord Buddha assigned one year to each of the animals.

Since then, these twelve animals have come to symbolise "The Twelve Earthly Branches" of the Ganzhi System, and have been universally acknowledged as being part and parcel of the Chinese calendar.

Thus when Chinese meet, merely by disclosing their "animal year" is sufficient for a fellow Chinese to know his/her age.

Indeed most Chinese do not ask for one's year of birth; rather the question is often phrased as "What animal are you ?"

The sixty year cycle comes about by combining the twelve animals with the five elements, Wood, Fire, Earth, Metal (or Gold) and Water.

The tables in Chapter Three present the corresponding animals and elements for the years 1900 to 1996 in accordance with the lunar calendar. Readers should note that the lunar calendar is divided into twelve months of 29 and 1/2 days each. Every two and a half years an extra month is added to "adjust" the calendar, and this extra month is consecutively interposed between the 2nd and the 11th months of the lunar year.

One of the important days of the lunar calendar is the so called "first day of spring" or as the people of Hong Kong refer to it, the "Lap Chun". Some lunar years have two "Lap Chuns", generally interpreted as being very auspicious, while other years may have no "Lap Chun" at all. A year without a Lap Chun is generally considered an inauspicious year especially for births and marriages.

The twelve animals are divided into the Yin (negative) and the Yang (positive) sides of the Earthly Branches.

Thus the Ox, the Rabbit, the Snake, the Sheep, the Rooster, and the Boar are on the negative side and are considered as Yin animals;

while the Rat, the Tiger, the Dragon, the Horse, the Monkey and the Dog are on the positive side and are considered as Yang animals.

The twelve animals have also each been assigned a compass direction. (See diagram next page).

COMPATABILITY
Based on these directions, "compatibility triangles", comprising three signs per grouping are established. Each of the three signs within the same triangle are believed to be compatible with the other signs because they generally exhibit the same types of characteristics.

The first grouping comprise the Rat (North), the Dragon, (E.Southeast) and the Monkey (W.Southwest). These animals are extremely "sympatico" with each other, and are thoroughly understanding of their own ambitious and impatient natures. Unions between these three animals are often long lasting and happy. Children and parents born of these three signs also get along extremely well with each other.

The second grouping is made up of the Ox ((N.Northeast), the Snake (S.Southeast) and the Rooster (West). These are the intellectuals of the Chinese Zodiac, the most dependable and the most determined. Marriages and partnerships between them are happy and successful.

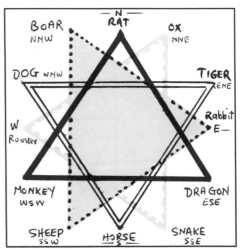

Compatability Triangles of the Twelve Animals

The third grouping comprise the Tiger (E.Northeast) the Horse (South) and the Dog (W.Northwest). These are the most idealistic of the Animal signs. They get along extremely well with each other.

The final grouping is made up of the Rabbit (East), the Sheep (S.Southwest) and the Boar (N.Northwest). These Animal signs are characterised by their compassionate and emotional natures. They are followers rather than leaders, and they are generally motivated by love and beauty rather than by material gains. They are exceedingly compatible with each other.

INCOMPATABILITY

According to the Horoscope, Animal signs which are placed diametrically opposite each other in the Compass are generally incompatible with each other. Combinations of this nature often result in direct clashes, with each eyeing the other as rivals and adversaries.
THUS: * The Rat clashes with the Horse.
    * The The Ox is in conflict with the Sheep.
    * The Tiger fights with the Monkey.
    * The Rabbit's adversary is the Rooster.
    * The Dragon's arch enemy is the Dog, and
    * The Snake cannot tolerate the Boar.

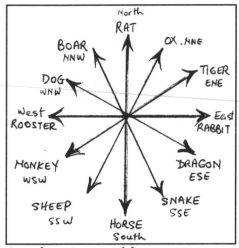

Animal Sign Incompatabilities

Each of the twelve animals also have certain characteristics and attributes, and at the first level of astrological analysis, they are said to enjoy good and bad years during a twelve year cycle depending on their intrinsic relationship with each other.

Thus, generally speaking if they are in conflict with each other, then they each experience unlucky periods during the years ruled by the sign that is in conflict with them. Similiarly, Animal signs enjoy relatively peaceful and fruitful times during the years that belong to signs with which they are compatible.

Subsequent levels of horoscope analysis suggest more complex evaluations, ie when the Hours of birth time, and the interactions of the five Elements are considered. Before going into that however it is useful to examine the characteristics, and the relative fortunes of each of the twelve animals in a twelve year cycle.

THE RAT

This is the first animal of the Chinese Zodiac. The Rat is a POSITIVE sign symbolising the direction NORTH, and the WINTER season.
The years of the RAT during the present century are the lunar years as follows:

** January 31st 1900 to February 18th 1901 **
** February 18th 1912 to February 5th 1913 **
** February 5th 1924 to January 24th 1925 **
** January 24th 1936 to February 10th 1937 **
** February 10th 1948 to January 28th 1949 **
** January 28th 1960 to February 14th 1961 **
** February 15th 1972 to February 2nd 1973 **
** February 2nd 1984 to February 19th 1985 **

The years of the Rat are generally pleasant ones for everyone. These are years characterised by good times and lots of wealth making opportunities. Most business endeavours started during Rat years will do well, especially long term type ventures. Rat years are seldom volatile, nor are there very many natural disasters.

People born during Rat years (and this generally also applies to countries) enjoy good times during the years of the Rat, the Ox, the Dragon, the Sheep, the Monkey, and the Rooster. They do not fare so well during the years of the Horse, the Dog and the Boar.
The Rat person's luck over a twelve year cycle is summarised here:

In the year of the RAT, the Rat will enjoy prosperity, promotion prospects and career advancement. Money will flow in easily and there will be few disappointments. This is a good time to enhance the Feng Shui of the home and office, as the Horoscope influence is positive and conducive to making improvements.

In the year of the OX, the Rat will enjoy moderately good luck. There will not be any major windfalls of money luck, but life is smooth and there will be some benefits from work and career. This is also a good year to make Feng Shui enhancements in the house to activate and create greater intensity of good luck.

In the year of the TIGER, the Rat person or country enjoys another average year. The year indicates some travel, some personal loss and some difficulties, but it is not a bad year. Feng Shui changes undertaken during the year will be beneficial.

In the year of the RABBIT, the Rat person could experience some loss of money. There could also be problems at the office and on the home-front, but these are troubles which will blow over. If the Feng Shui is right, those wanting additions to the family could succeed. Business opportunities could also present themselves.

In the year of the DRAGON, the Rat ejoys excellent fortunes. This is the year when both business and career will prosper; the Rat will also enjoy recognition and honours. Feng Shui enhancement of any kind this year will definately embellish the Rat's already excellent fortunes. It is only necessary to guard against being too trusting of new friends and/or business associates. Those who enjoy windfall profits this year should also be careful of over-spending.

In the year of the SNAKE, the Rat is still enjoying the euphoria of the previous year's successes. Some loss of money and disappointments however could cloud the previous year's gains. However, this is not a bad year, and things get back to normal by the year-end.

In the year of the HORSE, the Rat must face financial difficulties and exorbitant expenses. It is a year of indebtedness and lawsuits and there will be disappontments in matters pertaining to love and family.

In the year of the SHEEP, the Rat is once again poised for growth and further advancement. This is a year characterised by new opportunities and changes for the Rat, and any Feng Shui alterations to the house will be most beneficial.

In the year of the MONKEY, the Rat enjoys a continued spate of good fortune. No serious difficulties block his progress, apart from minor disagreements on the business or career front. This is generally a dynamic time for the Rat and once again, any Feng Shui alterations will be most beneficial.

In the year of the ROOSTER, the Rat enjoys yet another bonanza year. There is plenty of good news and fresh business developments. The Rat will also find himself the centre of attention during the year of the Rooster, enjoying much social success and prestige. The only caution is that he should guard against overwork and over confidence. It is also an extremely good idea to make whatever Feng Shui alterations needed during the year to "tap" the year's good luck and use it to "protect" the home and office from less fortunate years.

In the year of the DOG, the spate of good luck begins to taper. It is time now for the Rat to slow down and wait for his star to ascend again. Patience and spiritual strength is now called for as there will be misfortunes, relating to work and business. Feng Shui alterations should have been done the previous year, although the rat should definately check for hidden arrows which may be hurting his/her Feng Shui. Remember that in a bad year, unfortunate Feng Shui consequences do tend to get amplified.

In the year of the BOAR, the Rat continues his quiet period for another year. It is not a good time for new investments or changes of any kind, since this is a period when it is better for the Rat to consolidate, and continue to be patient.

THE OX

The Ox is the second animal in the Chinese Horoscope. It is a NEGATIVE sign and its direction is NORTH,NORTH-EAST. The Ox also symbolises the WINTER season.

The years of the Ox in the present century are the lunar years as follows:

** February 19th 1901 to February 7th 1902 **
** February 6th 1913 to February 25th 1914 **
** January 25th 1925 to February 12th 1926 **
** February 11th 1937 to January 30th 1938 **
** January 29th a949 to February 16th 1950 **
** February 15th 1961 to February 4th 1962 **
** February 3rd 1973 to January 22nd 1974 **
** February 20th 1985 to February 8th 1986 **

The years of the OX are generally years of hard work. Conservatism prevails and emphasis is focused on applying serious and conscious efforts towards work. Discipline and solid old fashioned atitudes and well tried formulae work better during Ox years than new creative ideas and methods. Ox years are also characterised by small conflicts and minor misunderstandings, which tend to get sorted out without too much difficulty.

People born in the years of the Ox generally enjoy excellent luck during the years of the Rat, the Ox, the Snake, the Monkey and the Rooster. The Ox experiences problems and have difficult times during the years of the Tiger and the Horse. The other years offer moderate good fortune. During the bad years it is advisable that the Ox does not introduce any Feng Shui changes. However, it does help for him to be observant of his surroundings and defend himself against any presence of poison arrows.

The Ox person's trend of luck over the twelve year lunar cycle are summarised herewith as follows:

In the year of the RAT, the Ox enjoys good fortune at work and at home. It will be a prosperous year; important recognition and new responsibilities are generally predicted.

This is an wonderful year for the Ox to "tap" into his good luck and to attempt new ventures. It is also a good year to improve his Feng Shui if he so wishes, as this will considerably magnify good fortunes.

In the year of the OX, the Ox continues to have a good year although it is not as spectacular as the previous year. It is however a year of "happy" occasions ie marriages or births or new additions to the family. Indeed family oriented events tend to take precedence during the year. Feng Shui changes undertaken will also be beneficial for the family.

In the year of the TIGER, the Ox experiences troubled times. Difficulties and obstacles appear frequently and unless care and vigilance are maintained this could be a year of grave problems of the most serious nature. Any Feng Shui improvements contemplated must be aimed at deflecting oppositions, danger and bad luck.

In the year of the RABBIT, the Ox's fortunes recover slightly, but it is still a mixed year. Problems continue to require attention and losses will be incurred. If it is a particularly bad year and the Elements are not in his favour, there could also be the loss of a loved one. Overall however the Ox will do averagely well during the year.

In the year of the DRAGON, the Ox continues to have a mixed year. There will be unexpected problems and developments which lead to annoying conflicts and difficulties although patience and hard work allows these problems to be alleviated. The year of the Dragon is not necessarily a completely bad year as there will be helpful mentors around as well. This is an excellent year for the Ox to introduce Feng Shui features into his home and office.

In the year of the SNAKE, the Ox enters a period of good fortune. Money flows in and business opportunities can be taken advantage of easily. This is a year also for expansion and growth for the Ox and any Feng Shui enhancements installed during the year will be beneficial.

In the year of hte HORSE, the OX once more becomes unsettled. An unhappy love life, emotional type problems and family troubles demand the Ox's attention. Accidents and poor health are also indicated, and financial affairs take a beating as well. Most of the bad luck takes place during the first half of the year however and by the close of the year things improve. It is not a good year to introduce too many changes to the house or office. Any Feng Shui being considered should best be left to the end of the year or to the following year.

In the year of the SHEEP, the Ox's confidence level takes a turn for the better as there is a fair amount of good news coming his way. This is the kind of year where no real tangible progress is made on any front, but peace prevails and there . are few problems to overcome. Feng Shui undertaken during the year will be beneficial.

In the year of the MONKEY, the Ox experiences abundant good fortune. It is an excellent year, overflowing with prosperity, goodwill, honour, recognition and even some fame. New business ventures, new partnerships, new careers, and promotions all come easily during the year. From a Feng Shui point of view this is an extremely good time to introduce new features that will enhance and magnify the year's predicted good luck. What this means is that the Horoscope indicates no conflict.

In the year of the ROOSTER, the OX's good fortunes continue. It will be a happy and enjoyable time marked by small joyful occasions. One or two small instances of betrayals and/or dishonesty could cloud the horizon but by and large it is a moderately good year. Feng Shui changes can be undertaken during the year.

In the year of the DOG, the Ox appears to be slipping into an unfortunate period, however it is not really a year of losses or bad luck since problems are only minor irritations rather than large and complex. In matters of the heart there appear to be some strains. This is not a very favourable year to introduce Feng Shui changes or for that matter to undertake any major renovation works. Better to wait till the following year.

In the year of the BOAR, the Ox will be extremely busy, with many activities and many people demanding his/her attention. However it is not a prosperous year, and financial matters enjoy only moderate good luck. It is however a good year for building for the future. This is an excellent year to introduce Feng Shui changes to the house or the office as the year is extremely conducive to long term type activities meant to benefit the future.

THE TIGER

The Tiger is the third animal in the Chinese Horoscope. Its direction is EAST-NORTHEAST and it symbolises the month of February in the WINTER season. The Tiger is a POSITIVE sign.
The following are the years of the Tiger:

** February 8th 1902 to January 28th 1903 **
** January 26th 1914 to February 13th 1915 **
** February 13th 1926 to February 1st 1927 **
** January 31st 1938 to February 18th 1939 **
** February 17th 1950 to February 5th 1951 **
** February 5th 1962 to January 24th 1963 **
** January 23rd 1974 to January 28th 1987 **
** February 9th 1986 to January 28th 1987 **

The years of the TIGER are volatile and dangerous years. These are years marked by wars and conflicts and when fierce natural and man made disasters of all kinds tend to occur. Tiger years are years when things happen on a grand and huge scale and where, for the most part, the stakes are high. These are also years of extravagant and high drama marked by flared tempers, intolerance and much snarling.

It is not a year that gives much assistance to the perpetuation of friendships, trusts and/or partnerships. Indeed, Tiger years are not regarded as the best times to start business partnerships, or attempts to forge strong alliances. far better to be patient and wait for the more benign and friendly influence of the Rabbit year that follows.

On the positive side, because of their intrinsic characteristic Tiger years succeed in forcing issues out into the open and this often has a "cleansing" effect, particularly on relationships and events. Thus although weak partnerships tend to be severed during the year of the Tiger, this is not always necessarily a bad thing for the parties concerned.

People born in the years of the Tiger generally enjoy robust good luck in the years of the Rabbit, the Horse, and the Sheep. Danger threatens them during the years of the Rat, the Ox, the Dragon, and the Monkey. The Tiger's trend of luck over the twelve year lunar cycle are summarised as follows:

In the year of the RAT, the Tiger faces business and financial difficulties. Plans for expansion and/or growth cannot meet with success. It is a year which calls for patience and consolidation, prudence and hard work. It is also not a good idea to introduce Feng Shui changes to the home or office.

In the year of the OX, the Tiger will experience quarrels and confrontations. There is a great show of stubbornness and ill tempers leading to a great deal of unresolved conflicts. Tiger people are warned to exercise a great deal of patience if this is not to turn into a disatrous year. Feng Shui changes are also not recommended during this year.

In the year of the TIGER, the Tiger's fortunes improve, but only marginally. He is lucky enough but only in the sense that he has access to assistance and help when he requires it. The time is still risky and fraught with dangers. Unexpected bad luck can still materialise. The Tiger is advised to check his Feng Shui during the year in order to install "protective" measures.

In the year of the RABBIT, the Tiger begins to come out of his bad period. There is good news on the horizon at last, and business interests and fortunes take a turn for the better. Obstacles and difficulties soon melt away and achievements are tangible. This is definately a good year. Any Feng Shui changes installed this year are beneficial.

In the year of the DRAGON, there is a slight reversal of fortunes. The year is a moderately good one but some kind of loss or unhappiness is also predicted. This is a very good year to install Feng Shui cures and features as they will be beneficial.

In the year of the SNAKE, the Tiger enjoys a peaceful period. There is steady progress and expansion although for some, matters of the heart could lead to a certain amount of restelessness. This is generally considered a moderate year when any changes motivated by Feng Shui awareness will be helpful.

In the year of the HORSE, Tigers enjoy an exceptionally brilliant time of great good fortune. Everything proceeds smoothly. It is a year marked by plenty of money and happiness. There is also plenty of good news, honours, recognition and opportunities. This is an excellent year to enhance the Feng Shui of homes and offices.

In the year of the SHEEP, the Tiger extends his run of good fortune, enjoying continuing success at work and in business. On the domestic front there might be some tension although nothing serious or disastrous is predicted. Feng Shui changes made during the year will be helpful in moderating mis-understandings on the home front.

In the year of the MONKEY, the Tiger experiences setbacks and disappointments. As this is not a good year, hostile confrontations are greatly discouraged. Instead Tiger people should exercise tolerance and patience, otherwise there could be unnecessary problems which could have been very easily avoided. This is not a particularly good year to install Feng Shui changes although the advice is to be wary of hidden poison arrows which can intensify the bad luck of the year.

In the year of the ROOSTER, the Tiger enjoys a mixture of good and bad news. All difficulties can be overcome and all problems can be solved satisfactorily although it may not appear so during the first half of the year. There is assistance from unexpected quarters and new partners/allies. This is also a very good year to introduce any Feng Shui changes which can enhance the Tiger's good luck.

In the year of the DOG, the Tiger enjoys a fairly good year. Once more he is helped by good friends and powerful people. There is little to complain about except that busy schedules and hardwork will demand more from the Tiger this year. However hard work does pay off as all plans and goals are attainable this year. It is thus a good year to be industrious. Feng Shui alterations made during the year will be beneficial.

In the year of the BOAR, the Tiger enjoys a great deal of money luck during the first half of the year, although this soon dissipates as the year progresses. A certain amount of caution is thus recommended. There is no gambling or speculative luck this year. Hence Tiger people should be cautious about punting in the stock market or investing in high risk business ventures. New projects must also be viewed with great caution. And certainly any apparent get-rich-quick ideas should be instantly thrown out ! Feng Shui alterations made during the year are very beneficial.

THE RABBIT

The Rabbit is the fourth animal in the Chinese Zodiac. Its direction is EAST and it stands for the month of March, symbolising SPRING. The Rabbit is a NEGATIVE sign.

The following are the years of the Rabbit:

** January 29th 1903 to February 15th 1904 **
** February 14th 1915 to February 2nd 1916 **
** February 2nd 1927 to January 22nd 1928 **
** February 19th 1939 to February 7th 1940 **
** February 6th 1951 to January 26th 1952 **
** January 25th 1963 to February 12th 1964 **
** February 11th 1975 to January 30th 1976 **
** January 29th 1987 to February 16th 1988 **

The years of the RABBIT offer peace and quiet after the turbulent years of the Tiger. Discretion, diplomacy and a more docile atitude describes the Rabbit years. Persuasion and a conciliatory approach towards work and relationships become the order of the day, and a more easy going atitude typifies much of the year's events.

There will be a tendency to avoid conflicts, side step difficult decisions and ignore disagreeable problems. Rabbit years reflect the animal's calm demeanour to the extent that leisure even takes precedence over work. On the business and money front, these are years which do not present too many predicaments or dilemmas. Lifestyles are casual and relaxed. The pace of the year is accordingly languid, with no tendency to speed things up. There is also no sense of urgency attached to decisions or problems.

Rabbit years are generally happy years with few matters of pressing urgency. Neither are there crisis situations that demand volatile or hurried responses. On the negative side, this laid back atitude can sometimes lead to over-indulgence and too much pampering.

People born in the years of the Rabbit are generally popular and easy going. They are also sensible, wise and full of good humour, and their atitudes are often positively coloured by their excellent manners and charming dispositions. Rabbit people are destined to lead fairly lucky lives. Their charts often predict good business fortunes and the possession of sharp and astute minds. Rabbit people enjoy excellent fortunes during the years of the Rabbit, the Horse, the Sheep and the Dog. Danger lurks during the years of the Ox, the Tiger, and the Rooster. The Rabbit's trend of luck over the twelve animal years are summarised as follows:

In the year of the RAT, the Rabbit enjoys a generally uneventful year with no unpleasant surprises and almost no difficult problems. Progress at work and in business is moderately steady, and within the family, there is domestic bliss and a general sense of well being. Feng Shui changes underatken during the year will be fruitful and beneficial

In the year of the OX, the Rabbit must be extremely wary as it will be a difficult time. The fortunes of the year are against the Rabbit; plans cannot succeed; health is bad; social interface is uncertain and there is also the possibility of the loss or the separation of a loved one. This is not a good year to make any changes to the home and any Feng Shui plans contemplated for the year should best be postponed.

In the year of the TIGER, the Rabbit is not yet out of danger. Extra care and precaution must be taken to guard against hostile conflicts and unreasonable demands made. This is also a year when there could be inconvenient and annoying lawsuits, mainly connected with business. Rabbits should be wary of executing important contracts or getting involved in business transactions. Feng Shui changes are not recommended except those pertaining to the installation of "protection" against poison arrows.

In the year of the RABBIT, the Rabbit is blessed with a great deal of abundant good luck. It is a very auspicious time. Careerwise there will be advancement and promotions. There will also be substantial money luck, with even the promise of unexpected windfalls. All business transactions go smoothly and honour comes to the family. There will also be flattering recognition from important people. Any Feng Shui alterations made during the year will be beneficial.

In the year of the DRAGON the Rabbit's good fortune generally continues. In fact the year is characterised by additional new advancement and the entre' of powerful friends into his/her social circles. There are few problems either at home or at work. It is also a good year to become aware of Feng Shui since any enhancements or alterations introduced will be beneficial. Indeed, this seems to be one of the best years for the Rabbit to introduce Feng Shui changes.

In the year of the SNAKE, the Rabbit's luck seems to be levelling. Difficulties and new problems begin to encroach upon the Rabbit's business and career. It is also a busy time as there will be many things to attend to. In some case a relocation of either the job or the business or the place of residence are indicated. This is not a bad year to undertake some Feng Shui alterations in order to safeguard against the problems of the year becoming too strong.

In the year of the HORSE, the Rabbit recovers his good fortune. There will be many good and helpful friends who enable the Rabbit to overcome diffcult problems carried over from the previous year. This is an excellent time to introduce Feng Shui features into the home.

In the year of the SHEEP, the Rabbit enjoys yet another very auspicious year. It is a year filled with abundance and with several money making opportunities. Prosperity and good health, happiness, and the attainment of plans are all indicated during the year. Again it is an excellent year to introduce Feng Shui features into the home.

In the year of the MONKEY, the Rabbit's luck is neither good nor bad. It is generally an uneventful and calm year, and while there might be minor hitches and some small problems, this is generally a good time to consolidate and take things easy.

In the year of the ROOSTER, the Rabbit is in danger of succumbing to financial difficulties and some grave misfortune. A great deal of care should be exercised, and if possible the help of others should be sought to overcome the tribulations of this period. Feng Shui Cures should be installed during the year to counter the bad luck of the year.

In the year of the DOG, the Rabbit solves the problems of the previous year, and while small obstacles remain, the Rabbit will not have to cope with too much frustrations. It is a good year to introduce Feng Shui changes, especially defensive measures which protect against betrayals by friends and/or business associates.

In the year of the BOAR, the Rabbit experiences some successes and some failures. There will not be very many trying situations but accomplishments are also limited. There could also be some unexpected difficulties cropping up suddenly. At best it is a mixed time for the Rabbit. Feng Shui changes introduced will however be beneficial.

THE DRAGON

The Dragon is the fifth animal in the Chinese Zodiac. It symbolises the EAST-SOUTH-EAST direction and stands for the month of April. Its season is SPRING. The Dragon is a POSITIVE. Dragon years during the present century are:

** February 16th 1904 to February 3rd 1905 **
** February 3rd 1916 to January 22nd 1917 **
** January 23rd 1928 to february 9th 1929 **
** February 8th 1940 to January 26th 1941 **
** January 27th 1952 to February 13th 1953 **
** February 13th 1964 to February 1st 1965 **
** January 31st 1976 to February 17th 1977 **
** February 17th 1988 to February 5th 1989 **

The years of the Dragon are often described as magnificent and spectacular; they are years of bravado and of great ambitious dreams. The Chinese attach special connotations to Dragon years deeming them excellent times for marriages· and births. Dragon children are highly prized, and businessmen often expand and start new ventures during Dragon years. There is a great deal of enthusiasm and energy, plenty of optimism and confidence.

Unlike the fortunes of the preceding Rabbit years, the years of the Dragon can be volatile and dramatic, sometimes strongly marked by massive natural disasters like floods and fires. Everything is magnified, be they successes or failures; honours or scandals.

People born in the years of the Dragon often reflect the temperamental, high energy characteristics often used to describe the Dragon. They are also supposed to be brave and courageous, strong are arrogant. In China the Dragon symbolises the emperor, and therefore takes on connotations of power and prestige; the Dragon is also regarded as a celestial creature, the only animal which can fly without wings. The Dragon is featured in Feng Shui lore as the Green dragon, and his breath is the all important cosmic Chi !
Dragon year people are thus expected to rise to high positions of power and authority and to enjoy great wealth and prosperity.

According to the Chinese Horoscope the Dragon fares well during the years of the Ox, the Dragon, the Snake, the Rooster, and the Boar. He has only one really bad year and that is the year of the Dog. During the other years, Dragon people enjoy moderately good periods of mixed fortunes.

In the year of the RAT, the Dragon has the chance to savour a great deal of good fortune. Money flows in easily and there is also romance in the air. There are no difficulties either at work or at home. There is also good Feng Shui luck during the year, and changes installed will be beneficial and fruitful.

In the year of the OX, the Dragon experiences another good and peaceful year when nothing goes wrong and most things go right Money progress, though not spectacular is steady and encouraging. The Dragon also succeeds in rising above the fray in the disputes and quarrels which swirl around him. Feng Shui also has the capability to further enhance the good luck.

In the year of the TIGER, the Dragon comes into conflict with this other volatile animal. It is a worrying and rough time. There is little progress made. Most plans and strategies are effectively blocked by obstacles. There are also potential adversaries who will make things difficult. However the Dragon does overcome all his difficulties. It is not a good year to introduce Feng Shui features into the home or office.

In the year of the RABBIT, the Dragon enjoys a fairly calm period characterised with few problems or difficulties. Home life and work life is settled and peaceful. There is no bad news and certainly no financial problems. It is a good year to enhance Feng Shui features in the home.

In the year of the DRAGON, the Dragon comes into his own and enjoys excellent and auspicious good fortune. All kinds of blessings and prosperity mark the year. Success comes easily and effortlessly. There is recognition and extreme high honours which takes the Dragon person on a "high". Confidence and optimism characterise the year and any Feng Shui features installed during the year will be of great benefit.

In the year of the SNAKE, the Dragon's good fortune continues. Everything proceeds smoothly, especially in business and commercial matters since the Dragon will be full of energy and vigour. In matters of the heart however this is only a moderately successful year. Feng Shui features introduced during the year will be favourable.

In the year of the HORSE, the Dragon has a moderately good year. There is some uncertainty which could lead to perplexing situations. There is also some bad news and some unpleasant developments. However on the whole this is not considered a bad year as all problems will eventually be worked out. Feng Shui changes can be made during the year.

In the year of the SHEEP, the Dragon experiences yet another mixed year with moderate gains achieved in career and work. There is minimal money luck but no real losses will be sustained. There could be some worries on the health side but these are not serious. This is also a fairly good year to introduce Feng Shui features into the home.

In the year of the MONKEY, the Dragon continues enjoying moderate growth. Business and financial matters however will achieve better performance than the previous year, although a certain amount of caution is also advised as there are messy legal battles predicted as well. Partnerships will be strained and even broken, and confrontional atitudes could escalate. Prudence and patience is thus advised. For Feng Shui changes this is not a bad time.

In the year of the ROOSTER the Dragon once again enjoys an auspicious year. There is happiness, career advancement, promotions, and money luck flowing in. It is also a year of powerful new alliances and friendships formed. An excellent year to enhance one's Feng Shui.

In the year of the DOG the Dragon experiences his worst year. This is a time for lying low, for keeping still and for avoiding all confrontations since one problem after another will beset the Dragon. Business ventures will also not be successful. At work there could be difficulties. Do not make any Feng Shui adjustments this year.

In the year of the BOAR, the Dragon comes out of his dark period and once more enjoys some good luck. Business and work proceeds smoothly and with some success. On the home front things are also peaceful and happy. Social life will be active and there is plenty of entertainment and pleasure travel indicated. Feng Shui features introduced during the year are beneficial.

THE SNAKE

The Snake is the sixth animal of the Chinese Zodiac. It is a NEGATIVE sign which symbolises the month of May. Its direction is SOUTH-SOUTH-EAST and its season is SPRING. The years of the Snake fall within the following dates:

```
**  February 4th 1905 to January 24th 1906    **
**  January 23rd 1917 to February 10th 1918   **
**  February 10th 1929 to January 29th 1930   **
**  January 27th 1941 to February 14th 1942   **
**  February 14th 1953 to February 2nd 1954   **
**  February 2nd 1965 to January 20th 1966    **
**  February 18th 1977 to February 6th 1978   **
**  February 6th 1989 to January 26th 1990    **
```

The years of the Snake are elegant years marked by flashes of wisdom and a great deal of diplomacy. The Snake's cool and serene approach to life is reflected in much of the year's elegant approach to situations. There will be a flowering of the arts and a greater conscious awareness of fashion and beauty. Romance and courtships bloom, and advances are also made in the sciences. It is also a good year for commerce and industry. Amidst all this ambience however there are under-currents of distrust and a certain amount of tension. Snake years are not tranquil years.

The Snake is the strongest of the YIN signs (negative) just as the Dragon is the strongest of the Yang signs (positive). While graceful and composed on the outside, the Snake conceals a mysterious and complex nature. Thus while on the surface events appear to proceed smoothly, there will be deeper and more profound motivations lurking beneath. Like the uncoiled spring of a striking snake whose bite is lethal and who moves as fast as lightning, disastrous events or changes during the year will be sudden and deadly. It is therefore wise to be wary. Stay away from speculation and gambling and consider carefully before investing in new and risky ventures.

Snake people are considered the most profound thinkers in the Chinese Zodiac. According to the Chinese Horoscope, they are often endowed with a mysterious wisdom and great intuitive powers. Snake people are generally born attractive and beautiful and are destined to rise above the social class in which they were born. Snake women are physically ravishing and usually lead charmed lives.

People born in the years of the Snake are advised to be careful and tolerant during the years of the Tiger and the Dragon. They have very auspicious good luck during the years of the Rabbit, the Monkey, the Rooster, the Dog and the Boar. Details of what they can expect in each of the lunar years are summarised as follows.

In the year of the RAT, the Snake person experiences many successes and setbacks. It is a busy period marked by advancement in careers and businesses, yet at the same time, there will also be losses and a certain amount of difficulty on the home front. However the Snake personality will be well equipped to sail through the year and come out better than at the beginning. It is a good year to introduce Feng Shui features to the home and office.

In the year of the OX, the Snake's fortunes continue on along a moderate path. There will be irritations at work and in business dealings, but once again things come right in the end, even though some losses could be sustained. It is a good year to introduce Feng Shui features into the home.

In the year of the TIGER, the Snake continues to be irritated by a series of small but annoying mishaps, problems and opposition. It is not a good time for the Snake and care is advised when dealing with people. This is a year when discretion is the better part of valour. Feng Shui changes will be beneficial.

In the year of the RABBIT the Snake has to tolerate a busy and hectic schedule of events and meetings which seem to take up all his/her time. Generally though, this is a happy year when friends and relatives visit. Feng Shui changes introduced during the year are beneficial.

In the year of the DRAGON, the Snake has to brace himself for tough times. This is a year marked by scandals and gossip, losses and danger. Business cannot advance. Careers are stymied and problems "come not in ones and twos but in battalions". Snake people are advised to lie low during the years of the Dragon, conserving strength and energy for the good times ahead. The year's bad luck eases towards the end of the year which brings some good news.

In the year of the SNAKE, the Snake native plans and strategises; calmly investigating his options and making solid plans for the future. This is not a flamboyant time for ostentatious enjoyment. Rather it is a period when the serious side must take control in order to build a sound base for the future. Feng Shui features introduced during the year wil be beneficial and fruitful.

In the year of the HORSE, The Snake's fortunes improve considerably. His well laid plans begin to show encouraging results, and any difficulties or problems are shortlived. Friends come forward to assist. Romance is also in the air and despite initial setbacks, the Snake's emotional life during the year will be happy. It is a good year to introduce Feng Shui changes.

In the year of the SHEEP, the Snake is protected from disastrous losses and/or betrayals. This is a time when he will make influential friends and tie up new contracts which will bring success at a later stage. This is an excellent year to introduce Feng Shui changes.

In the year of the MONKEY, the Snake recieves a lot of assistance from friends and unexpected quarters; and he needs all this help because it is a year of conflicts and disputes. Not a good time to install Feng Shui chnages to the home.

In the year of the ROOSTER the Snake enjoys a tremendously auspicious time. Achievements will be fantastic and honours will come easily. Promotions, wealth, and excellent results flow inwards. This is the best year for the Snake. Profits will be large and incomes will expand. Altogether an extraordinarily good year. An excellent time for Feng Shui to be introduced.

In the year of the DOG, the Snake continues having excellent opportunities to shine brilliantly especially at work and in careers. There is travel, a great deal of fun and also some romance. This is a good time to introduce Feng Shui.

In the year of the BOAR, the Snake's run of good luck continues. It will be a busy year, and hectic. There will be a few minor setbacks and the Snake needs to be careful but by and large, there will be more gains than losses. Any Feng Shui features introduced during the year will be beneficial.

THE HORSE

The Horse is the seventh animal in the Chinese Zodiac. It's direction is SOUTH and it represents the month June. Its symbolic season is SUMMER and it is a POSITIVE sign. The years of the Horse in the lunar calendar fall within the following dates:

** January 25th 1906 to February 12th 1907 **
** February 11th 1918 to January 31st 1919 **
** January 30th 1930 to February 16th 1931 **
** February 15th 1942 to February 4th 1943 **
** February 3rd 1954 to January 23rd 1955 **
** January 21st 1966 to February 8th 1967 **
** February 7th 1978 to January 27th 1979 **
** January 27th 1990 to February 14th 1991 **

The years of the Horse reflect this noble animal's free spirit. These are years of high adventure and swift enterprise, when calculated risks can be taken and the promise of upward mobility and career advancement exists. It is also a time when people and organisations can successfully push for greater efficiency and productivity. For some there will be much feverish activity demonstrating high energy levels. It can thus be an exhausting time.

Rationalisation and excuses will generally tend to get shoved aside as the action oriented characteristics of the year push for decisions to be made, for projects to get started and for plans to move ahead. It is a time of enhanced confidence, sound common sense and good humour. These are years when those who wish to strike out on their own into entreprenuerial ventures should take the plunge since the Horoscope is in favour of this kind of boldness.

People born in the year of the Horse are usually friendly and well disposed towards others. They have cheerful personalities and are socially popular. The Horse also possesses a streak of independence and tends to be impatient. They can acquire wealth and become incredibly successful, but are also big spenders. The Chinese believe that the Horse (like the Tiger and the Dragon) are strong masculine signs more suited for males.

The Horse experiences good times in the years of the Rabbit, the the

Horse, the Monkey and the Dog. The years of the Rat and the Boar will be difficult years. Details of the fortunes of the Horse in the twelve lunar years are summarised as follows.

In the year of the RAT, the Horse will experience bad luck in the form of money troubles and instability in his love life. There wil also be confrontations with the law and severe loss of money. It is altogether a time of adversity for the Horse, when prudence, discretion and patience are called for. It is certainly not a good time to introduce Feng Shui features.

In the year of the OX, the Horse's luck improves slightly, Times are still difficult but some monetary gains and small successes temper the predicaments of the year. This is a good year to introduce Feng Shui features into the house and office as they will be beneficial.

In the year of the TIGER, the Horse's luck begins to get better. It will be a happy time when love and family life blossom. It is also an active period characterised by a lot of socialising and entertaining. But the Horse tends to get over confident and arrogant in this kind of scenerio which could lead to disputes and misunderstandings. On the money side there is not much advancement indicated. Feng Shui changes may be made during the year.

In the year of the RABBIT, the Horse will have a great deal of auspicious fortune coming his way. There is, in particular plenty of money luck. Investments will be fruitful; decisions made lead to smooth operations within the business and careers, and there is genral advancement indicated. This is also a year for marriages and births, and any Feng Shui features introduced into the home or office will definately be beneficial.

In the year of the DRAGON, the Horse experiences a fairly depressing time typified by a certain amount of instability and uncertainty. Lack of confidence and a sense of pessimism will tend to prevail. The Horoscope does not however, indicate a bad time, and outcomes are generally predicted to be lucky rather than unlucky. There is thus no neccesity to fret. This is a good year to introduce Feng Shui into the home or office.

In the year of the SNAKE, the Horse is destined to have to work quite hard to overcome the difficulties of the year. There will be problems and entanglements, caused largely by partners and friends. This is not a fortuitous year and at best complications can be sorted out but there will be little or no progress or advancement made.

In the year of the HORSE, prosperity and great good fortune comes to the Horse ! At last his troubles are behind him. The Horoscope indicates all kinds of good things; ie promotions, advancements, recognition and a great deal of money luck. Since this is such a good year, the Horse must not sever ties with any of his allies, nor should he be over confident. It is a very good year to install Feng Shui features as these will be beneficial.

In the year of the SHEEP, the Horse continues to have good fortune. A major trip overseas is indicated which could lead to a relocation for several years. This is also a calm period where there will be none of the dramatic problems of previous years. Good Feng Shui can be successfully installed during the year.

In the year of the MONKEY, the Horse experiences yet another lucky and auspicious year, this time with indications of an unexpected windfall. Money luck is very good this year, and domestic life is peaceful and happy. This is also a good year to introduce Feng Shui changes.

In the year of the ROOSTER, the Horse has a moderate year. Family life is happy and peaceful while working life is not beset with any major problems. Small irritations throughout the year do occur but these are minor in their overall influence. It is a good time to undertake Feng Shui improvements.

In the year of the DOG, the Horse student enjoys tremendous good fortune, as it is a time of exceptional good luck for examinations, scholarships or academic awards. Respectability and recognition are indicated. A very good year. Feng Shui changes to improve the alignment of homes and offices are encouraged this year, mainly to try and counter the bad luck of the following year.

In the year of the BOAR, the Horse is forced to come down to earth as he will have to grapple with enemies and hostile forces. Unexpected difficulties and obstacles will force changes and cause setbacks to plans. This is altogether a rough year for the Horse, and certainly not a time to enter into new contracts or investments.

THE SHEEP

The Sheep (also refered to as the Goat) is the eighth animal in the Chinese Horscope. Its direction is SOUTH-SOUTHWEST, and it symbolises the season SUMMER. The month it signifies is JULY. The Sheep is a Negative sign. Years of the Sheep are between the following dates:

** February 13th 1907 to February 1st 1908 **
** February 1st 1919 to February 19th 1920 **
** February 17th 1931 to February 5th 1932 **
** February 5th 1943 to February 24th 1944 **
** January 24th 1955 to February 11th 1956 **
** February 9th 1967 to January 29th 1968 **
** January 28th 1979 to February 15th 1980 **
** February 15th 1991 to February 3rd 1992 **

羊

The years of the Sheep are quiet and generally peaceful. The pace slows down after the frenetic energies of the preceding Horse years. Much of the year's focus will centre around the family. Careers and commercial enterprises tend to take a back seat as the influence of the Sheep shifts attention towards a flowering of more artistic and cultural pursuits. There is a rediscovery of the great benefits of harmony and tranquility.

This is not a year of confrontations or conflicts. This is a year when conciliatory sentiments will take precedence. It is generally a year of peaceful pursuits and restful introspection.

People born in the year of the Sheep are generally mild mannered, kind and honourable. It is regarded as the most feminine of the twelve animal signs, and is thus thought to possess more of the generally accepted "feminine" characteristics including a tendency towards being sentimental and emotional. Sheep people prefer staying at home to going out, favour giving in to fighting, and usually frown on anti-establishment type behaviour. He has a tendency to be negative but loves anything beautiful and creative. The Sheep generally prefers leisure to work.

The Sheep person will enjoy good times during the years of the Rat, the Snake, the Horse, the Monkey and the Rooster. There will be distressing periods during the years of the Ox, the Sheep and the Dog. The fortunes of the Sheep in the twelve years of the Animal Cycle are summarised as follows:

In the year of the RAT the Sheep enjoys outrageously good fortune, and is blessed with a great deal of speculative luck. Gains will be made from lotteries, gambling and even investment in high risk ventures. Plenty of sound commercial ventures are also indicated. There is also considerable happiness indicated in the area of love and romance. Altogether a quite spectacular year, very suitable for Feng Shui features to be installed.

In the year of the OX, the Sheep must be wary as this will be a distressing year marked by arguments and conflicts. This is also a very unlucky year and all the gambling luck of the previous year seems to have vanished into thin air. Severe financial difficulties are generally predicted for the year. This is a year to lie low.

In the year of the TIGER, the Sheep has to cope with extended family problems and conflicts with relatives, especially those connected with inheritance matters. There will be opposition and contentious haggling, and life is not smooth. Apart from this however, work-days and careers run smoothly. Feng Shui features introduced during the year will be beneficial.

In the year of the RABBIT, the Sheep might have to deal with setbacks and problems related to family matters. Relatives will give him a difficult time. However this is not considered a bad period and by the end of the year, circumstances resolve themselves, with the Sheep making positive headway in settling dilemmas. This is a good year to introduce Feng Shui features into the home.

In the year of the DRAGON, the Sheep is much sobered by the problems of the preceding two years. There is a reduction of significant confrontations during the year, but money luck is only average. The Sheep needs to lie low and live a quiet life for peace and harmony to be restored. This is not a good year to introduce Feng Shui features or undertake renovation work of any kind since the year is not conducive to making major changes.

In the year of the SNAKE, the Sheep regains much of his lost vigour and confidence. This is an auspicious year marked by the recovery of all that was lost in the previous two years ... and more ! Honours and awards, power and prestige and high position are indicated as definate possibilities during the year. Any bad news or setbacks will be temporary. This is an excellent year to introduce good Feng Shui features as they will be beneficial.

In the year of the HORSE, the Sheep's good fortune continues. It is a mild and serene year. No major misfortunes occur. There is money and business luck. Troubles which plagued him in the past no longer cause any problems. This is indeed a very good time. Feng Shui alterations to the home or office will be beneficial.

In the year of the SHEEP, the Sheep experiences a moderately lucky period. While not as fruitful as the previous two years, this period marks a return to popularity and a happy social life. Commercial enterprises cannot succeed, and expectations must be curtailed. Feng Shui changes may be introduced during this period.

In the year of the MONKEY, the Sheep attracts auspicious fortune once again. Advancement and promotion chances are bright. This is an excellent period of rewards and fruitful investments.
There is a multiplicity of agreeable bonuses which mark the year's progress. It is also a good time to install Feng Shui features into the home and office to effectively enhance the good fortune.

In the year of the ROOSTER, the Sheep's run of "good luck years" taper off. This is a time when fresh conflicts and irritations occur and finances take a beating. Enemies also emerge and there is need to be careful. Socially the Sheep's popularity does not diminish, but excesses are costly. Not a good year to install Feng Shui features.

In the year of the DOG, the Sheep will suffer some major setbacks. Huge debts pile up. Family troubles are distressing. Investments bring problems and generally almost all areas of business, work and family demonstrates the manifestation of this year's bad joss. Health will also not be good. It is not a recommended time to commence renovations.

In the year of the BOAR, the Sheep experiences distressing times. It continues to be a year of distrust and discord. Friends and business associates as well as subordinates and bosses tend to be uncooperative. Home life is unhappy. Only finances show slight improvements. Not a good time to install Feng Shui features.

THE MONKEY

The Monkey is the ninth sign in the Chinese Horoscope. Its direction is WEST-SOUTHWEST and it represents the month August. Its season is SUMMER. It is a POSITIVE sign. The years of the Monkey fall within the following dates:

** February 2nd 1908 to January 21st 1909 **
** February 20th 1920 to February 7th 1921 **
** February 6th 1932 to January 25th 1933 **
** January 25th 1944 to February 12th 1945 **
** February 12th 1956 to January 30th 1957 **
** January 30th 1968 to February 16th 1969 **
** February 16th 1980 to February 4th 1981 **
** February 4th 1992 to January 22nd 1993 **

The years of the Monkey are happy and highly creative years marked by a lot of fun and games. Ventures deemed impossible take off smoothly. There is a great deal of mergers and acquisitions activity in the world of commerce and high finance. And also some scandals !

According to the Chinese, the Monkey symbolises cunning and agility, intelligence and creativity. Years symbolised by the Monkey generally see an expansion in the number of astute deals and shrewd money making activities. There is a sense of optimism and confidence, and the feeling that "nothing is impossible". There is however, a great deal of bravado, and the year will generally be carried along a tide of headlong expansion. Risky and speculative ventures will be in vogue, with the year favouring those who are nimble and quick-witted.

People born in the year of the Monkey are charming and full of guile. They are generally refered to as quick witted geniuses and are bright, adaptable and resourceful. The Monkey is a very positive person, a touch arrogant and sometimes filled with a sense of his own importance. He is also extremely manipulative and energetic. His personality is bright and sparkling and highly entertaining but never make the mistake of underestimating him !

Monkey year people usually do extremely well during the years of the Rat, the Rabbit, the Dragon, the Monkey and the Rooster. Difficult times beset hin during the years of the Tiger, the Dog and the Boar.

Details of how the Monkey's fortunes fluctuate according to each of the years in the 12 year cycle are summarised as follows:

In the year of the RAT, the Monkey enjoys an auspicious period. There is much merry-making with money flowing in easily. It is also a fantastic time to expand and to make requests of others as it is a year when almost nothing goes wrong. All problems are minor and get solved easily. Popularity soars. This is an excellent year for marriages, births and introducing Feng Shui adjustments.

In the year of the OX, the Monkey's aspirations and ambitions are somewhat hindered by the slower pace of the year. His fortunes, while still good are not as brilliant as the previous year and progress slows down. There could even be some loss experienced and annoying outbreaks of illness. It is a good year to install Feng Shui changes, especially defensive measures to guard against the bad luck of the following year.

In the year of the TIGER, the Monkey goes through a most unpredictable period. It is generally regarded as a bad time for Monkeys and most Horoscope source books indicate this as a period when the Monkey could succumb to his/her enemies. It is definately a year of weakness and vulnerability when just about everything that can go wrong will. Better then to to be patient and passive.

In the year of the RABBIT, the Monkey's fortunes improve considerably. Coming out of the trauma of the previous year the Monkey will find himself with mentors and surrounded by a lot of helpful people, and although progress is not spectacular either at work or in the business, it is an amelioration of the troubles suffered last year. On the domestic front things also move smoothly. This is a good time to introduce Feng Shui changes.

In the year of the DRAGON, the Monkey enjoys prestige and honour from his peers and gains some superiority in his immediate environment. However despite the obvious progress in status, it is not a peaceful year. There are worries over relationships, and expenses will be very high. It is not a year to be overly aggressive in expansion plans. Feng Shui features introduced during the year will be beneficial.

In the year of the SNAKE, the Monkey's ambitions get welcome help and assistance from mentors and powerful people. This is regarded as an excellent year for business expansion, when plans can be implemented quite smoothly despite minor irritations caused by dissensions at home. It is a good year to install Feng Shui changes.

In the year of the HORSE, the Monkey must live on his wits and be something of a political animal if he is to manoeuvre himself out of the tight situations he will find himself embroiled in during the year. It is however a lucky year with little or no major crises to hamper future growth. This is also a good year for Feng Shui features to be introduced as they will be beneficial.

In the year of the SHEEP, the Monkey enjoys excellent luck in business and career. These are busy times marked by much entertaining and socialising. There will also be more travel required than usual. A word of caution. There could be unforeseen setbacks and predicaments during the year caused by unscrupulous or dishonest people. A good year to install Feng Shui features.

In the year of the MONKEY, the Monkey native reaps excellent gains and profits. This is a very good year where there is a great deal of happiness and much advancement. The Monkey will be full of energy and vigour during the year and all plans move along smoothly. Definately a good year to install Feng Shui changes as they will be beneficial.

In the year of the ROOSTER, the Monkey continues with his good luck. Money luck continues to be good and helpful people are still around. Marriage and lovelife suffer some distress. There will also be some opposition from people causing strife and conflict. Feng Shui defensive measures are recommended to guard the next two years.

In the year of the DOG, the Monkey's luck turns bad. There will definately be some loss of money and investments will go sour. Friends prove to be "fairweather". Disappointments mount up through the year and it is best to lie low and stay quiet. It is not a good time to make Feng Shui adjustments this year. Be very careful !

In the year of the BOAR, the Monkey's difficulties do not dissipate. Law suits and financial problems will plague him: his health will deteriorate. This is a very bad year for the Monkey & he has to suffer humiliations and defeat. No one can be trusted and all partnerships and joint ventures in business will prove to be dangerous. Be patient.

THE ROOSTER

The Rooster is the tenth sign in the Chinese Horoscope. It's direction is WEST and it symbolises the start of AUTUMN, signifying the month of September. The Rooster is a NEGATIVE sign. The years of the Rooster fall within the following dates:

**   January 22nd 1909 to February 9th 1910   **
**   February 8th 1921 to January 27th 1922   **
**   January 26th 1933 to February 13th 1934   **
**   February 13th 1945 to February 1st 1946   **
**   January 31st 1957 to February 17th 1958   **
**   February 17th 1969 to February 5th 1970   **
**   February 5th 1981 to January 24th 1982   **
**   January 23rd 1993 to February 9th 1994   **

The years of the Rooster tend to be as optimistic as the years of the Monkey but with less of the Monkey's creativity and guile. Rooster years are periods when business and commerce tend to encounter irritating complications made worse because of unnecessary fuss. There is also more noise than real substance, more empty promises than genuine profits or good ideas. Confrontations are usually not serious, and quarrels will usually blow over. Much of the events of the year will centre around pomp and ceremony rather than real achievements.

Rooster years however are generally bouyant years and are usually indicative of improving fortunes for most people. Indeed the Rooster years are generally predicted to be times when there will be enough food and sustenance for everyone.

People born in the years of the Rooster are usually proud and arrogant. There is always an air of dignity about them that is quite distinctive. Roosters possess many qualities associated with efficiency and performance, and many of them are destined to shine in life because of their many outstanding qualities.

They also have a tendency to be very good with money and with budgeting, and are generally loyal and trustworthy. Roosters normally make the best business partners, but they love being applauded and are very allergic to criticism.

Roosters shine most during the years of the Tiger, the Dragon, the Snake, the Sheep, the Rooster and the Dog. They have to endure hardships and some adversity during the years of the Rat and the Horse. There will also be worries during the year of the Boar.

In the year of the RAT, the Rooster is forced to face severe financial strains due to unforseen committments. Health and home life also suffer disturbances. Colleagues and friends cannot be relied upon for assistance of any kind and it is generally a trying time. It is not a very favourable moment to introduce Feng Shui changes.

In the year of the OX, the Rooster recovers lost composure suffered during the previous year. Outside help arrives at the doorstep and finances improve. The Horoscope indicates some kind of operation or loss of blood but the year is generally regarded as a relatively good one. Feng Shui installations will be beneficial.

In the year of the TIGER the Rooster will have an exciting period. There is a great deal of money luck and business investments bear luscious fruit. In fact it is such an auspicious year that opportunities keep knocking at his door. The advice is not to be over optimistic. Feng Shui discovered and introduced into the house this year will be beneficial.

In the year of the RABBIT the Rooster must definately not be over ambitious. Nor should he be too trusting or participate in speculative ventures. While it may not be a bad time, there is also a scarcity of good luck, so that it is better to lie low.

In the year of the DRAGON, the Rooster enjoys an excellent period of auspicious good fortune. Success shines on the Rooster as the spotlight is centered on his achievements and his abilities. This is also a year when power and authority are thrust on him. It is definately a great year to introduce Feng Shui into the house or office.

In the year of the SNAKE, the Rooster's good luck continues. It is a year for the Rooster to enjoy the fruits of the previous year's accomplishments. There will also be positive consolidation. Once again it is an excellent year for Feng Shui changes.

In the year of the HORSE, the Rooster's run of good luck come to temporary halt. It is a difficult time as there will be many obstacles and conflicts during the year. Plans go awry a great deal of the time forcing re-assessments and re-calculations. In relationships this is also not a good time. There will be quarrels with loved ones and also with office colleagues and co-workers. In a worst case scenerio, the Rooster may succumb to the manipulations of unscrupulous people. Thus there is a need to be careful.

In the year of the SHEEP, the Rooster enjoys the protection of powerful people. Most all of the problems of the previous twelve months are overcome or are dissipated. There is even time to devote to more domestic occupations and to engage in more leisurely pursuits. This is an excellent year to examine the Feng Shui of the house or office.

In the year of the MONKEY, the Rooster is faced with financial difficulties which will be annoying but not lethal. Events will subsequently show that things are not as bad as they first appeared. Misunderstandings with loved ones could lead to some unhappiness and there could be problems on the home front. By and large however the year's fortunes is at best moderate. It is however a good year to install Feng Shui features.

In the year of the ROOSTER, the Rooster native will make a spectacular revival. His fortunes will take a sharp turn for the better. There enters the presence of extremely powerful and influential people into his working life; people who will support his ideas and be instrumental in his advancement. This is therefore considered an excellent year. It is also a good time to introduce Feng Shui into the home.

In the year of the DOG, the Rooster's fortunes are once again excellent. Anything lost in the previous years will be regained. This is a very good follow up year. Popularity soars. Business is good. only in his personal life will there be some unhappiness. Good year to install Feng Shui features.

In the year of the BOAR, the Rooster will suffer bouts of depression and worry. Some kind of betrayal from close friends or associates is predicted or there will be some kind of personal disappointment. This is not a very good time to change the Feng Shui of the home or office. Better to wait a couple of years.

THE DOG

The dog is the eleventh sign of the Chinese Horoscope. It signifies the direction WEST-NORTHWEST and represents the season AUTUMN. It is a POSITIVE sign.

The years of the Dog lie within the following dates:

** February 10th 1910 to January 29th 1911 **
** January 28th 1922 to February 15th 1923 **
** February 14th 1934 to February 3rd 1935 **
** February 2nd 1946 to January 21st 1947 **
** February 18th 1958 to February 7th 1959 **
** February 6th 1970 to January 26th 1971 **
** January 25th 1982 to February 12th 1983 **
** February 10th 1994 to January 30th 1995 **

The years of the Dog sustain mixed predictions, with combinations of good and bad news. According to Chinese Zodiac descriptions, the Dog symbolises honour and fidelity, fairness and justice. Lofty virtues of patriotism and loyalty will get a sound hearing during the years of the Dog, but it is also a time when the determination and stubbornness of strong willed people will carry the day. Forceful minded dictators generally succeed in getting their way.

It is also speculated that this could be a year of confrontations and conflicts, chaos and insurrections. The outlook for some could be bleak, with prospects of strenuous and difficult times. There will also be an abundance of worry and constant bickering within relationships and between nations. Despite these annoyances however it is not an unstable period since the Dog also symbolises balance and equilibrium.

People born in the year of the Dog are generally stead-fast and reliable. They also make genuine friends and are usually known for their loyalty and honesty. The Dog is forthright and frank but tends to view the world within narrow limits and pigeon-holes, leaving little room for flexibility and "grey areas". This sometimes manifests itself in acute dogmatism bordering on stubborn-ness. Dog people are eternal pessimists. Though capable of great personal charm and warmth, they tend generally to be cold and unemotional in their working life.

They are the cynics of the Zodiac, forming attachments at a snails pace; yet once their confidence is gained you have a friend for life !

People born in the years of the Dog enjoy excellent times during the years of the Rat, the Tiger, the Snake, the Horse and the Dog. They generally experience difficulties and face hardships in the years of the years of the Dragon and the Rooster. Details of his fortune in the twelve years of the cycle are summarised as follows:

In the year of the RAT, the Dog enjoys successes in business and makes excellent profits from investments. This is a good year to introduce Feng Shui features into the home or office as the time favours changes and attempts to improve fortunes.

In the year of the OX, the Dog must face up to difficult decisions. There will be misunderstandings which arise within relationships with friends and colleagues. Good intentions are not appreciated and not understood. It is better to lie low and not attempt to ameliorate potentially explosive situations as the time does not favour amicable settlements. It is not a good year to make Feng Shui changes.

In the year of the TIGER, the Dog's personal relationship problems of the previous year eases. There is a reduction in conflict situations. Some trouble within the family occurs, but these blow over by year end. Feng Shui features installed during the year will be beneficial.

In the year of the RABBIT, the Dog enjoys spurts of excellent breaks. Business and commerce are generally predicted to prosper and there is money and partnership luck. There is advancement and general promotion indicated and problems are at a minimum. It is a good time to introduce Feng Shui features as they will be beneficial, particularly defensive type Feng Shui which protect against "poison arrows".

In the year of the DRAGON, the Dog must come to terms with misfortunes and adversities. This will be a trying and tiresome time with the prospect of loss of money, loss of face and perhaps also a loss of position. The Dog's Horoscope predicts the presence of dangerous adversaries. Stay cool and keep a low profile !

In the year of the SNAKE, the Dog's fortunes take a sharp upswing. The problems of the previous year will all be resolved satisfactorily. This is his year ! There will be support from powerful people and money and financial luck as well. It is also a good time to install Feng Shui features to tap into the good luck of the year.

In the year of the HORSE, the Dog's auspicious period continues. This is a year of expansion and development. Good progress is made on all fronts. This is probably his best year in the cycle and he should try to make the most of it. Petty problems should be shoved aside. Concentrate instead on consolidating and strengthening any gains made during the year Feng Shui changes will bring benefits.

In the year of the SHEEP, the Dog's confidence is shaken with the onslaught of some setbacks. This is nevertheless a fairly good year although with little of the preceding year's spectacular luck. It is however, not an unfortunate period. Losses can be avoided and obstacles can be overcome.

In the year of the MONKEY, the Dog enters a relatively calm period where things move smoothly and satisfactorily. There is no outstanding good luck indicated but there is no bad luck either. Family life will be happy and settled. This is an excellent year to make Feng Shui changes.

In the year of the ROOSTER, the Dog must cope with problems of an emotional nature. There could be significant areas of conflict between friends and colleagues, and in some cases legal disputes could materialise, creating predicaments and perhaps even mushrooming into severe problems. The year's luck is only moderate and losses suffered during the year could very well be permanent.

In the year of the DOG, the Dog enters into the protection of his own sign. If he is lucky the losses of the previous year can be recovered. Whatever the outcome of disputes the Dog will emerge from the year a stronger person as valuable lessons are learnt. This is a "safe" year but it is also not a great year. Stay patient. If Feng Shui features are installed this year they will be beneficial and effective.

In the year of the BOAR, the Dog enjoys a peaceful period when there is respite from the difficulties of the previous years. There will be no major problems surfacing unexpectedly, but there will also not be anything spectacularly successful either. This is a year best spent on recuperating, making new friends and regaining strength. It is a good year to introduce Feng Shui onto the house or office.

THE BOAR

The Boar (or PIG) is the last animal in the twelve year cycle of the Chinese Horoscope. The Boar signifies the month of NOVEMBER and the season of AUTUMN. It is a NEGATIVE sign.
The years of the Boar fall within the following dates:

** January 30th 1911 to February 17th 1912 **
** February 16th 1923 to February 4th 1924 **
** February 4th 1935 to January 23rd 1936 **
** January 22nd 1947 to February 9th 1948 **
** February 8th 1959 to January 27th 1960 **
** January 27th 1971 to January 15th 1972 **
** February 13th 1983 to February 1st 1984 **
** January 31st 1995 to February 18th 1996 **

The years of the Boar are generally years of goodwill and abundance. The business environment will be conducive to impressive profit making opportunities and commerce and industry tend to flourish. These will be lucky years for those who do not prevaricate but instead proceed with their plans and are action oriented.

There will be a general feeling of ambience and extravagance during the years of the Boar. Social life and activities will be on the upswing. Parties, celebrations and the pursuit of leisure activities will be more pronounced than work; the danger then is the prospect of overdoing things. Extravagance could lead to financial problems while over-indulgence could lead to excesses.

People born in the years of the Boar are usually nice simple folk whose view of the world is superficial and are coloured only by his jovial and care free personality. Boar people are usually extremely kind hearted and amiable, compassionate and generous. But also fairly frivolous in their outlook of life. The Boar loves pleasure and leisure ! Not for him the obsession to amass a huge fortune or a hankering for power and prestige. This is definately one of the less ambitious signs of the Zodiac.

The Chinese Horoscope predicts a generally uneventful life for the Boar. Most years his luck will be moderate and fair, with little or none of the high drama of some of the other more volatile signs. The Boar does well and enjoys very good luck during the years of the Ox, the Dragon and the Horse. There will be extremely difficult times during the years of the Rat, the Tiger and the Dog. Details of his fortunes over the cycle are summarised as follows:

In the year of the RAT, the Boar faces uncertainties and predicaments. It is a moderate year in that bad luck and good luck occur in fairly equal measures. There is a tendency towards depression and worries but problems can be overcome, It is a good time to install Feng Shui changes as they will be beneficial.

In the year of the OX, the Boar's luck is predicted to be excellent. This is a year when he can trust his intuition and his own judgement as business investments bear fruit quickly and surely. There is a great deal of money luck. However matters of the heart may suffer some annoying setbacks. This is a great year to install Feng Shui features.

In the year of the TIGER, the Boar is forced to face adversity on his own. He will be plagued with severe financial difficulties and it is a very tough year. The Boar needs to be extra wary of trusting people close to him in his work. This is also a time when he cannot depend on others. He is very much alone ! This is a bad time for Feng Shui changes.

In the year of the RABBIT the Boar's gains are modest and slow. Nevertheless some welcome progress is made ! There is also the promise of financial successes towards the end of the year. Family life is happy and contented. This is a good year to introduce Feng Shui into the household.

In the year of the DRAGON the Boar's life is destined to move ahead smoothly and happily. Powerful and influential friends offer assistance and support, and there are also prospects of public recognition. A couple of tiny losses occur but these do not detract from the spectacular good luck that will be felt during the year. It is an excellent time to install Feng Shui features as they will be beneficial.

In the year of the SNAKE, the Boar's good fortunes continue but at a much lesser pace, and with some minor financial problems. There are some difficulties indicated which impact on the harmony of the family unit causing annoying distractions. There could also be sad news about a member of the family. Not a good time for Feng Shui.

In the year of the HORSE, the Boar's fortunes are excellent. There will not be any speculative or gambling luck, but business and finances will generally have no problems. There is advancement indicated for those with careers or those undertaking important examinations and interviews. From the viewpoint of beginnings this is an excellent year. Thus new ventures, new jobs and new partnerships are all favoured. Similarly this is an excellent time to introduce Feng Shui into the home or office.

In the year of the SHEEP, the Boar's financial situation comes under some strain. Money luck is not very good. However, for those in working life, there could be promotions and upward mobility in their careers. This is the kind of year which favours planning and careful study of situations or new projects rather than the conception of headlong changes. It is a good year to discover Feng Shui !

In the year of the MONKEY The Boar's financial situation does not improve. The problem of over-indulgence and "living beyond his means" continues ! The Boar should guard against succumbing to temptations of making "easy money" or participating in speculative high risk ventures. Indebtedness of some kind is generally indicated for the year.

In the year of the ROOSTER the Boar's money luck does not see any major improvements. Home life and career enjoy a moderately peaceful period but lack of money will be felt as a major obstacle and a major source of frustration during the year. This is not a bad time to introduce Feng Shui features into the home as it will be beneficial.

In the year of the DOG, the Boar faces another potentially difficult year. There will be problems from all over and in every sphere of his life ie at work, at the office, in the home and in his relationships with people; it is a year of frustration and depression. Be patient. This is not a good year to install Feng Shui changes.

In the year of the BOAR, the Boar's luck at last begins to show some signs of improvement. Money matters begin to stabilise and progress is made to improve his finances. Minor disputes continue to occur but by and large the luck has modified. The Boar will see some good news during the year. This is a good time to introduce Feng Shui changes into the house or office as a means to improve the luck over the coming years.

THE 12 SIGNS AND THE HOURS

The relative personality characteristics and fortunes of the 12 signs are also influenced by the times of birth. The Horoscope divides a 24 hour day into twelve categories of two hours each, and further assigns one of the "animals" to each of these twelve divisions. This tabulation is reproduced here for easy reference:

THE ANIMAL SIGN	THE HOURS
THE RAT	11 pm - 1 am.
THE OX	1 am - 3 am.
THE TIGER	3 am - 5 am.
THE RABBIT	5 am - 7 am.
THE DRAGON	7 am - 9 am.
THE SNAKE	9 am - 11 am.
THE HORSE	11 am - 1 pm.
THE SHEEP	1 pm - 3 pm.
THE MONKEY	3 pm - 5 pm.
THE ROOSTER	5 pm - 7 pm.
THE DOG	7 pm - 9 pm.
THE BOAR	9 pm - 11 pm.

Thus, although the animal symbol of the YEAR of birth generally "rules" the fortunes of people, the Chinese Horoscope also takes note of the animal which is in ascendant during the HOUR of birth. This extra dimension of analysis suggests that a person's personality traits are generally modified according to this HOUR of birth ie a Dragon person born in the hour of the Boar will also exhibit some Boar characteristics.

Similarly the HOUR of birth also tempers the more extreme predictions and forecasts given under the Horoscope's yearly categorisations. Generally, in matters of divination there is quite a good deal of subjective judgement and interpretation involved. Readers are strongly advised to refer to the Horoscope only to obtain a general guide of "trends of lucks" rather than to look for specific predictions.

THE 12 SIGNS AND THE ELEMENTS

In addition to exercising direct influence on FENG SHUI the Elements and Element Analysis also plays a pivotal role in the unveiling of predictions under the Chinese Horoscope system. Under the system each of the twelve Animal signs are assigned an Element based on the year in question. Since there are 5 Elements ie Metal (or gold), Water, Wood, Fire, and Earth, the 12 Animals and these 5 Elements when combined, form a 60 year cycle. The entire cycle for this century which "matches the Animal to the Element" in each of the years has been reproduced in the four tables named Table 1 in Chapter 3.

Element Analysis based on the Productive and Destructive Cycles apply in the same manner to the Horoscope as to Feng Shui and readers are encouraged to refer to that section for further insights into Element interactions. The interactions of the Elements with the 12 Animals generally result in modifications of character traits and predictions. Details of this modification are however beyond the scope of this book. The general characteristics of the Elements as they apply to Man are summarised as follows:

METAL: People born in Metal years tend generally to be independent, rigid, uncompromising, cold and unbending. They are usually very ambitious and determined people, preferring to trust their own instincts and judgements. Metal is controlled by Fire and in turn controls Wood.

WATER: People born in Water years are skillful orators and are extremely articulate and persuasive. They are flexible and intuitive and have none of the rigidity of Metal people. Water is controlled by Earth and in turn controls Fire.

WOOD: People born in Wood years are highly ethical, righteous,and exude great self confidence. They are born leaders, are progressive, generous and have excellent organisational abilities. Wood is controlled by Metal and in turn controls Earth.

FIRE: People born in Fire years are decisive, clever, creative, rational, popular and possessed of a fierce intellect. They are usually adventurous and courageous, and are born winners. Fire is controlled by Water and in turn controls Metal.

EARTH: People born in earth years are extremely practical and down to earth. They are also solid citizens, very systematic, organised and usually dependable and disciplined. Earth is controlled by Wood and in turn controls Water.

Postscript

... closing notes from the author

Attempting to convey something of the intensity of the wisdom that provide the philosophical underpinnings of Feng Shui in a book such as this, can at best only be partially successful, especially when viewed within the perspective of the vastness and sheer magnificence of mystic knowledge one is dealing with.

The exercise compels me to confront the certainty that the reader's span of concentration on the more academic aspects of the ancient texts ought not to be burdened with too much that is unfamiliar. Indeed, much of the theoretical complexities attached to the inter-relationships of the various ancient Chinese symbols that comprise the primary basics of Feng Shui represent a real challenge to the modern-day mind. Consequently it has been necessary to employ a certain amount of repetition.

Such reiteration is necessary for a thorough understanding of and sensitivity to the underlying principles. The full understanding of Compass School Feng Shui especially, requires solid groundwork in these areas. Only thus will the practice of the formula be sufficiently comprehensive. Once understood however, interpreting and analysing the "rules" and guidelines of Feng Shui become extremely engrossing and most certainly rewarding. This observation, I must add, is based very much on personal experience and observation.

In the beginning I viewed much of the explanations given by Feng Shui Masters with a great deal of scepticism. This cynicism notwithstanding, I continued to observe and to experiment. And of course I followed Feng Shui advice as well. It was, after all, always a no loss situation !

I have also been in possession of my personal Lo-Shu best and worst directions for many many years now, and with the benefit of hind sight have observed its incredible potency each time I "bothered" to activate these orientations. Because of course, through the years, my interest in, and practise of Feng Shui has waned and soared according to my fortunes at each moment in time. Nevertheless, I have long since developed the habit of always "checking my directions" in whatever I do, and wherever I live. A tiny compass also accompanies me wherever I go.

However, it was only after I made serious efforts to understand the background of Chinese thought, in the process delving deeply into the theories and philosophies of ancient sages, that much of Feng Shui began to make tremendous good sense to me.

This coincided with the time I was transferred to Hong Kong.

Since then Feng Shui's many facets, and its different interpretations have triggered an intellectual curiosity in the subject where before I had practised it on a merely "just in case " basis. In this I believe my atitude simply reflects my Chinese mind, ie I am a great believer of doing what I can to activate good luck !

When I tentatively suggested to Master Yap that we could perhaps pass on the formulas of the Pa-Kua Lo-Shu school of Feng Shui as a follow up to my introductory first book on the subject, I only half expected him to say yes. My experience with Feng Shui Masters in Hong Kong and Taiwan had taught me to expect a certain amount of reticence and reluctance when it comes to actually obtaining comprehensive explanations of complicated formulas, techniques and methodologies.

Master Yap's ready and generous acquiscence made this book possible. I am more than touched by his generosity of spirit, not only in magnanimously and universally sharing his knowledge, but also that he went to great pains to translate, and then to patiently explain the very complex and sometimes apparently "conflicting" insights given in the ancient text. In every single case of doubt or ambiguity however, the solution always presented itself after much discussion and debate, and when this happenened the particular "rule" or guideline in question became blazingly clear. Those were moments of sheer delight and undiluted pleasure, as we penetrated the veil of the language and the symbolism locked within the ancient words !

I have taken the liberty of simplifying as much of the text as possible especially as it pertains to the use and applications of the formula. Much of the appendices relating to landscape Feng Shui have been left out of this book since a great deal of it has already been covered in my first book. Where I have felt elaboration of related symbolisms and background information was necessary, I have devoted space to them, and in almost all such instances I have supplemented the relevant chapters with additional research from other sources.

One of the greatest joys of being a writer is the opportunity it creates to briefly touch the lives of others. It is a tremendously exhilarating and also a deeply humbling experience. And so, to the many readers of my first book who have made the effort to communicate with me, I dedicate this follow-up book of Feng Shui to you.

May it truly make a real and positive difference in your lives !

Lillian Too
Kuala Lumpur. July 1993.

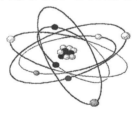